IDITAROD

THE GREAT RACE TO NOME

**PHOTOGRAPHY
BY JEFF SCHULTZ**

TEXT BY BILL SHERWONIT

Foreword by Joe Redington, Sr.
Preface by Susan Butcher

Alaska Northwest Books™
Anchorage • Seattle

Copyright © 1991 by Jeff Schultz and Bill Sherwonit

Alaska Northwest Books™, a division of GTE Discovery Publications, Inc., is independent of the Iditarod Trail Committee and it is not attempting in any way to associate itself with that committee.

Library of Congress Cataloging-in-Publication Data
Schultz, Jeff, 1960–
     Iditarod : the great race to Nome / photography by Jeff Schultz ; text by Bill
Sherwonit ; foreword by Joe Redington, Sr. ; preface by Susan Butcher.
          p.   cm.
     Includes bibliographical references (p. 142) and index.
     ISBN 0-88240-411-3
     1. Iditarod Trail Sled Dog Race, Alaska.   I. Sherwonit, Bill.
1950–   . II. Title.
SF440.15.S38   1991
798'.8—dc20   91-12909
                                                                                                    CIP

Edited by Ellen Harkins Wheat
Book and cover design by Alice Merrill Brown
Photo editing by Carrie Seglin
Cartography by David Berger
Typography by Phyllis Grossman

PHOTO CREDITS: All photographs by Jeff Schultz, except the following: William Ansely Collection, Alaska State Library: page 26. The Anchorage Museum of History and Art: 18, 19, 22, 23, 24, 27, 30, 36, 39, 40. The Vide Bartlett Collection, Album #3, Alaska and Polar Regions Dept., University of Alaska Fairbanks: 32–33. Copyright 1946 Jim Brown: 31, 35. Museum of History and Industry, Seattle, Wash.: 14–15, 16, 17, 21, 28, 41. Special Collections Division, University of Washington Libraries: 23, 25.
COVER PHOTOS: *Front cover:* As the first light of day casts elongated shadows, Lavon Barve's team travels up the Yukon River near Grayling in 1989. *Back cover:* A musher drives through a ravine in the Alaska Range during the 1985 Iditarod.

Alaska Northwest Books™
A division of GTE Discovery Publications, Inc.
22026 20th Avenue S.E.
Bothell, WA 98021

Printed in Hong Kong

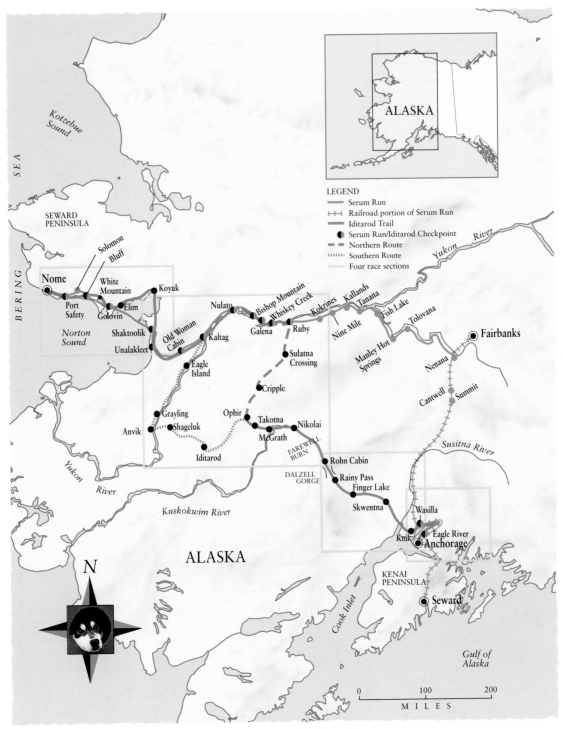

The Iditarod Trail

Foreword

Joe Redington, Sr., "Father of the Iditarod," takes his dogs on a training run near his Petersville Road training camp. Mount McKinley towers overhead.

YOU KNOW, I FEEL THAT a lot of things depend on luck, and certain things lead to other things, which is probably the reason that we need this book—to show people why we have an Iditarod race, how it began, and what it's all about.

Some of the best times of my life have been on the Iditarod Trail, whether I was working, training, or racing. I don't worry about anything, and it's a great feeling to be there with the dogs, watching them trotting along, their little old feet moving fast, and everything quiet as you whiz down the trail. It may be a night when the northern lights are bright, flashing from one part of the horizon to the other, or a beautiful sunrise, with the warmth of the sun so great after a good, cold night. It's a feeling that you have to experience to believe. It's funny, but most of the people who run the Iditarod, no matter how rough they've had it, want to go back and do it again.

In the two weeks that you run the Iditarod, you learn more about yourself than you ever knew before. You get time to think about the joys and sadnesses of life. I love to travel with a person who can laugh, even when you're standing together in water up to your knees at 30 below.

Someone who says, "Damn, what do I do now?" And 30 minutes later, you're going down the trail together, warm and happy again. You're looking for the adventure that's probably one of the greatest things you ever did in your life.

You meet so many fine people out on the trail who are dedicated to the race and the trail itself. Friends that you meet out there, you may not see for a whole year, but they're overjoyed to see you again, and you feel great visiting with them and telling them some of the adventures of the past year. It's a whole education in two weeks.

People always seem to be there when you need help on the trail. I recall one time, I was traveling between Kaltag and Unalakleet at night, and I fell asleep on the sled. I hit a tree and it knocked me off the sled, broke my light, and the dogs took off. There I was, crawling around on the ground, trying to fix my light. I finally figured out which way the dogs were going and I staggered after them. About 100 yards down the trail, they had stopped, which is something they seldom do. I was bleeding pretty badly, but I started down the trail. I hadn't gone a mile before I saw a bright light. It was two nurses camped on the trail, mushing for fun. One of them washed off the blood and patched me up, and I was on my way again, feeling great. But I was a terrible-looking sight when I got into Nome. These days, I guess I'm known for falling asleep on my sled.

Even with the struggle you can face in the race, the satisfaction and pleasures stand out so much that, until I can't keep up, I'll never stop mushing on the Iditarod Trail. It's been my highway for the last 40 years.

During the initial years of the Iditarod race, I met Jeff Schultz. I realized immediately that he was a talented photographer. He became our official race photographer, and since then he's done an excellent job of capturing the spirit of the race and the other "Idita" events. Since he always seems to be around when I do something stupid, I'm hoping someday that he will run the Iditarod so he can see what it's like from my end of the sled. I feel good about getting Jeff involved with the Iditarod. We gained a top photographer and I gained a real good friend.

I've often dreamed about a book telling the story of the Iditarod, how it started, what it means to so many people, how important the trail is to Alaska. That's why I was glad to hear that Jeff Schultz and Bill Sherwonit had decided to put one together. With Jeff's pictures and Bill's words, the book is sure to tell the true story. Both these men have a real feeling for Alaska. Their combined talents do justice to Iditarod and all the people who have been involved along the trail.

— *Joe Redington, Sr.*

The
Iditarod
Trail

The Gold Rush Era

SOME SEGMENTS of the race course followed by Iditarod entrants were developed centuries ago by Eskimos and Athapaskan Indians, long before Alaska was "discovered" by European explorers. Russian fur traders used portions of the route during the early 1800s. But without question, the Iditarod Trail's heyday was during the Territory's gold rush era, from the late 1880s through the mid-1920s.

Primarily a winter pathway (in summer, the swamps, bogs, and lowland tundra it crosses are virtually impassable), the trail acted as a transportation and communication corridor connecting mining camps, trading posts, and other settlements that sprang up during the gold rush. Serving as one of Alaska's main overland routes from 1911 into the early 1920s, the Iditarod was actually a network of trails. Its main stem started at the ice-free port of

Left: *Sled dog teams were often used to haul firewood, equipment, gold ore, and mail.* Above: *The largest gold nugget ever found in Alaska, weighing 97 ounces, taken from Anvil Creek near Nome in 1901.*

Nome residents pose with dog teams on the frozen Bering Sea in May 1906.

Seward and ended at the gold-boom town of Nome on the Bering Sea coast. Including side branches, the entire system measured more than 2,200 miles.

The southern portion of the route was created during the late 1880s, through what was known as "Cook Inlet country." Interestingly enough, the earliest trailblazers came seeking coal, not gold. The region's first notable gold strike was made at Resurrection Creek in 1891, and within five years more than 3,000 people had poured into the district. A second rush into the region occurred in 1898. Thousands of stampeders eventually settled in such Cook Inlet communities as Hope, Sunrise, Knik, and Susitna.

That same year, on the shores of the Bering Sea, prospectors found the gold-bearing sands of Cape Nome, thus triggering one of the biggest stampedes in U.S. history. Within two years, an estimated 30,000 fortune seekers set up camp, more than $2 million was extracted from Nome's "golden sands," and the city built a reputation as a wild West town characterized by claim jumping, violence, and corrupt officials.

As with most stampedes, many of the gold seekers failed to strike any riches at all. By 1905, Nome's population had dropped to about 5,000, but the town remained the commercial and communications hub of Northwest Alaska. Because of its regional importance, territory officials sought to end Nome's wintertime isolation, which often stretched from October to June when the Bering Sea was frozen and contact with the "outside" world was essentially cut off. After several attempts failed to establish a direct and economical overland route from Nome to ice-free ports in the state's Southcentral region, the U.S. Army's Alaska Road Commission ordered that a route be surveyed from Seward to Nome. Led by Walter Goodwin, a four-man team began the survey in January 1908 and in three months blazed a path hundreds of miles long.

In his survey report, Goodwin concluded that the proposed route would make sense economically only if additional gold discoveries were made along the route, thus increasing the amount of traffic. In an ironic twist, such a discovery occurred several months later. On Christmas Day 1908, prospectors W. A. Dikeman and John Beaton found gold on a tributary of the Haiditarod River, about 60 miles southwest of the route Goodwin had blazed—a strike that prompted Alaska's last major gold rush.

Malamute huskies were used as sled dogs in winter and pack dogs in summer.

By 1912, more than 10,000 fortune hunters had been lured to the so-called Inland Empire. Most settled in either Ruby or Iditarod (derived from the Indian word *haiditarod,* meaning a far distant place), but numerous other gold-boom towns and camps were established and connected by a crude system of trails. The Iditarod strike and subsequent gold boom prompted completion of the Seward-to-Nome project. A work crew of nine men and six dog teams—again led by Goodwin—cleared, marked, and improved nearly 1,000 miles of trail during the winter of 1910–11.

Through the mid-1920s, thousands of people traveled the Iditarod's network of trails in winter. Most drove dog teams, but some rode on horse-drawn sleds. Others walked, snowshoed, or even bicycled, usually because they couldn't afford to own or rent a dog team. One such hiker, Charles Lee Cadwallader, recounted his 1917 adventures in the book *Reminiscences of the Iditarod Trail.* "The dog team was an expensive thing to possess if you did not have work for them other than pulling you over the trail," Cadwallader said. As proof, he quoted the following prices: $200 for a "good" five-dog team; $150 for sled and harnesses; and

Mushing

The English word "mush" comes from the French *marche*, literally "to march." In *Racing Alaskan Sled Dogs*, F. S. Pettyjohn describes the origins of the word: "'Mush' has been used for at least 150 years, but the phrase 'dog musher' is quite recent. Up until the first part of the twentieth century, a dog musher was known as a 'dog driver' or a 'dog puncher.' To him 'mush' meant to 'move out,' but the old sourdoughs often used it to mean travel by walking or snowshoeing. Going from village to village was referred to as 'mushing.' Travel by dog team was called 'sledding' or 'dog sledding' or, more recently, 'dog mushing.'"

Modern sled dog drivers rarely use "mush." More common starting commands are "hike" or simply "let's go."

50 cents per dog per day to feed the team (or about $35 for a two-week journey with five dogs).

Cadwallader chose to walk from Anchorage to Iditarod in April. He explained: "At this time of year a person would not need snowshoes and would not experience any extreme cold. Ten below zero to 20 above zero would be the average temperatures to expect. The time it would take to mush in to the camp [a distance of about 400 miles] would require 12 to 20 days."

Traveling with several different companions, he walked anywhere from 14 to 62 miles per day. Though the pace was exhausting, he enjoyed the adventure: "This trail winding its way over the frozen tundra held something for the musher that outweighed his thought of being tired and every muscle being crowned with a boil. . . . This was the land of the midnight sun and it held romance. . . ."

The length of Cadwallader's daily travels, as for nearly everyone who used the trail, was determined by the distance between roadhouses. Dozens were established along the trail that connected Nome and Seward. According to the Bureau of Land Management (which in the 1980s prepared a management plan for the historic trail): "Almost as fast as the trail was surveyed, enterprising young men and women began staking out sites. . . . Those that were actually built and utilized were spaced about a day's journey apart [from 14 to 30 miles]. These inns were vital . . . for they meant a warm fire, shelter, and a hot meal after a day on the trail." All roadhouse owners were required to keep lists of their guests, to help track any who got lost.

Though prospectors, trappers, freighters, missionaries, government officials, and assorted other business people traveled the trail, one group earned special acclaim for their cold-weather heroism: mail carriers. Until dog teams were replaced by airplanes in the 1920s and '30s, mushers who owned mail routes were "kings of the trail." Not only did U.S. laws require that mail teams be given the right of way, but carriers also received special treatment at roadhouses. They typically were given the best seats at the table, the first servings of food, and the best bunks for sleeping.

Mail carriers earned such pampering: their job was a difficult and hazardous one. They frequently fought blinding blizzards, frigid temperatures, and 70-mile-per-hour winds to deliver the mail on schedule.

Pete Curran, Jr., delivered mail from Solomon to Golovin on the Bering Sea from 1924 to 1938. Running a team of 21 to 23 dogs (enough to get up hills while carrying 500 to 600 pounds of mail), Curran was expected to maintain a regular weekly routine from late November to early May:

three days to Golovin, three days back to Solomon, one day of rest, then back to Golovin. The challenge came in meeting that schedule in all kinds of weather.

"You'd have to be on time regardless of the weather or trail conditions," Curran recalled. "If I lost a day, I had to make a double run the next day. So I had to go no matter what the weather. . . . Sometimes in those storms you couldn't see half of the team. You just had to trust your leader to keep going."

Billy McCarty, who carried mail along the Yukon River between Ruby and Nine-Mile Point, recalled, "There were days the poor dogs, they just hated to go. Going upriver, against a headwind, cold; oh, it really bothered them. But we had no choice. They had to go, whether it was cold, or raining, or anything. They just had to go." For their services, mail carriers were paid as much as $150 per month, "a lot of money in those days, when things were cheap," McCarty said. "Back then, it was like $100,000. Good money."

Mail carriers weren't the only mushers to build heroic reputations along the Iditarod Trail during Alaska's gold rush days. Some of the era's most famous drivers were sled dog racers. During the trail's heyday, highly publicized mushing contests were staged at several gold-boom towns, including Iditarod and Ruby. But the greatest race of that era was born in Nome: the All-Alaska Sweepstakes.

Dog drivers delivered mail during Alaska's gold rush era. The team bears the "U.S. Mail" insignia.

The Gold Rush Era

ALL ALASKA SWEEPSTAKES, NOME, APRIL 8TH 1911.
ALLAN AND DARLING ENTRY AT THE POST.

The All-Alaska Sweepstakes

UNTIL THE EARLY 1900s, Alaska's mushers traditionally used dogs strictly for work or transportation. Drivers had little opportunity for recreation when they harnessed up their teams. Sled dogs were occasionally raced to settle a bet or determine the fastest team in the camp, village, or neighborhood. But there was no major competition—complete with official rules, judges, trails, and purse—until 1908, when a group of Nome sled dog owners staged the first All-Alaska Sweepstakes.

It makes sense that an isolated gold-boom town literally at the end of the trail would spawn what is now recognized as Alaska's official winter sport. With mining operations shut down for the winter, Nome's residents had plenty of time for long and sometimes heated discussions about one of their favorite topics—dogs. Drivers spent hours debating the relative merits of their

---

Left: *Crowds line Nome's Front Street for the start of the
All-Alaska Sweepstakes sled dog race in 1911.*
Above: *Three-time winner Scotty Allan.*

A handler holds a sled dog prior to the start of a race in Nome during the early 1920s.

Iditarod: The Great Race to Nome

teams. Finally, a miner and dog driver named Scotty Allan offered a solution to the unending debates. He suggested a race.

Born in Scotland, Allan Alexander "Scotty" Allan was lured to Alaska in 1893 by gold, but he found his riches in mushing. Even before Nome's historic race, Allan was recognized as one of the best dog drivers in Alaska.

But before focusing on Scotty's achievements, we need to give credit where it's due. Truth be known, it was Allan's six-year-old son, George, who first proposed a race to settle an argument about which family owned Nome's top dogs. George and his schoolmates organized a race for boys nine and younger. With a rather scruffy and then still unknown dog named Baldy for his leader, the younger Allan won the seven-mile, three-dog event. Nearly everyone in town attended the race, and local merchants offered prizes to the top finishers. Soon mushing replaced skating and skiing as Nome's favorite sport for both boys and girls.

With the younger set having so much fun, it was only a matter of time before adults agreed to resolve their dog debates in a similar fashion. It was Scotty Allan who said, "There be only one way to settle this thing: do like the lads do. [Have] a race to prove it."

Following Allan's lead, a lawyer and dog lover named Albert Fink made an inspirational speech to Nome's top mushers: "As I see it, such races will become a permanent thing in Nome. We all know what an important part dogs have contributed to the development of Alaska, how dependent we are up here on them for transportation. I propose that we establish a Kennel Club, the purpose of which will be to improve the strains of Alaskan dogs, and to better their conditions. The Annual All-Alaska Sweepstakes races . . . will serve to prove which dogs are best. I predict that dog racing in Alaska will prove as popular a sport as horse racing in Kentucky."

After forming the Kennel Club, with Fink as their president, Nome's

An entrant in a Ladies' Day Race drives her team through the gold-boom town of Iditarod in 1914.

dog drivers went about the task of organizing the first All-Alaska Sweepstakes. With Allan's guidance, the club settled on a 408-mile course from Nome to Candle and back, along a trail that would cross a variety of terrain, including sea ice, mountains, rivers, tundra, and timber.

To ensure that contestants would follow a code of fair play and take proper care of their dogs, the club instituted a set of regulations that have served as the basis for modern race rules. Among the most notable:

• The cruel and inhumane treatment of dogs by any driver is strictly prohibited under penalty of losing the race and forfeiture of the team.

• Each team must take all of the dogs with which it started to Candle and return to Nome with the same dogs and none others.

The racers were obliged to return with every dog, dead or alive. Therefore, it was to every driver's obvious advantage to treat his dogs well, so that he wouldn't have to carry the extra weight of a dead or disabled dog on his sled. To prevent illegal substitutions, the Kennel Club photographed each dog and recorded its name, color, and markings.

To arouse public interest in the Sweepstakes, the club staged short races during the fall and winter of 1907–08. And Fink raised $10,000 in prize money, to be split among the top finishers. The strategy worked perfectly. By race day in April 1908, a holiday spirit enveloped the town.

A Sweepstakes queen and her court were elected, and Nome's schools and courts closed on race day. Most businesses were shut down, but one establishment that remained open—and filled to the seams—was the Board of Trade Saloon, which served as race headquarters. People went there for race updates, and also to place their bets; hundreds of thousands of dollars changed hands.

The marathon event started and finished on Nome's Front Street. Its route followed a telegraph line to Candle, and messages could therefore be relayed back to headquarters. Bulletins on the race leaders and the condition of men and dogs were periodically posted throughout Nome.

Ten teams entered the inaugural Sweepstakes. The first driver to leave the chute, Paul Kjegstad, drove his own team, although it was more common for a team owner to pick a driver. Thus John Hegness, the winning musher, drove a team owned by Albert Fink. His winning time for the 408-mile race was 119 hours and 15 minutes. Scotty Allan settled for second place.

Teams left the starting line at two-hour intervals, a practice that proved unfair. Because of the long wait between starts, the final team left 18 hours after the first and some mushers drove into storms that others missed entirely. So in succeeding years, the starting interval was decreased to 15,

A bulletin board posted in Nome's Board of Trade saloon summarizes race information for the 1913 All-Alaska Sweepstakes. The winning entry, driven by Fay Delezene and owned by a man named Bowen, is circled in the lower left-hand corner.

WINNERS FIRST ANNUAL ALL-ALASKA SWEEPSTAKES, NOME, ALASKA.

John Hegness, driving a team owned by Albert Fink, won the inaugural All-Alaska Sweepstakes with a time of 119 hours and 15 minutes.

10, and five minutes. Finally, in 1912 and future Sweepstakes races, teams left one minute apart to minimize the weather factor.

The second Sweepstakes attracted 13 mushers and was marked by several racing innovations. In winning the 1908 race, Hegness had run a mail-dog team, complete with freighting harness and sled. But the following year, Allan used a sleeker, lighter sled—weighing only 31 pounds, it was the forerunner of the modern racing sled. He also used simpler harnesses that allowed the dogs greater freedom of movement.

Aided by his refined gear and again driving a team owned by J. Berger, Allan won the 1909 race despite getting caught in a severe blizzard. It was during this storm that Baldy—whom Allan had once considered a mediocre mongrel—proved his championship mettle. Baldy somehow found his way through the whiteout and led Allan's team into the winner's circle. Within days, Scotty Allan was being heralded in headlines around the world as "King of the Arctic Trail." His scruffy leader, meanwhile, had earned the title "Baldy of Nome."

Despite Baldy's heroics, not all of Nome's attention was focused on the winning entry. The third-place team, driven by Norwegian immigrant Louis Thrustrup and owned by a Russian fur trader named William Goosak, earned considerable notoriety by using Siberian huskies. These dogs were much smaller and lighter than the big, powerful freighters used by most Sweepstakes contestants. Fox Maule Ramsay, another Nome miner and dog driver, was so impressed that he traveled to Siberia the following summer and purchased several of the small huskies. In 1910,

Iditarod: The Great Race to Nome

he entered three teams of Siberians in the Sweepstakes. One of those teams was driven by John "Iron Man" Johnson, who finished the 408-mile event in 74 hours, 14 minutes, and 37 seconds—a speed record that was never broken. Ramsay, driving his own set of Siberians, placed second.

The Siberian imports gained enormous popularity and became the sled dogs of choice through the remainder of the Sweepstakes series. But several mushers, Scotty Allan among them, stayed with more traditional Alaskan sled dogs, including malamutes and Native-bred huskies, setters, pointers, collies, hounds, Airedales, or some combination of hounds and huskies. Allan had little reason to change dog breeds after the 1910 race. Five of his 10 dogs had been injured when the team tumbled down a 200-foot cliff, yet the team still managed to finish third.

Scotty and Baldy returned to the top in both 1911 and 1912, strengthening their positions as kings of the North. Fay Delezene won the Sweepstakes title in 1913, and Iron Man Johnson earned his second victory in 1914 with Allan taking second.

The 1914 Sweepstakes marked the first appearance of Leonhard Seppala, who was destined to become an even greater mushing legend than Scotty Allan. Born and raised in Norway, Seppala had also come to Alaska in pursuit of gold. But soon after arriving in Nome, he began working as a dog puncher. The sled dog racing fever that swept Nome in the early 1900s eventually infected him, and he entered his first Sweepstakes at age 37. The race was traumatic for Seppala. His team of Siberian huskies got caught in a storm and lost the trail. Then, while searching for the route along the coast, his team nearly ran off a cliff. Eventually, with several dogs suffering from cut feet and lost toenails, he dropped out.

Then came the 1915 Sweepstakes, and the start of the Seppala legend. The race favorite was, as usual, Scotty Allan. But Seppala, competing in only his second major race, outmushed the acknowledged master and placed first. Many more victories followed, in Nome and elsewhere. Seppala won the next two Sweepstakes races, before the event was discontinued in 1918 because of World War I. In a racing career that would span 45 years, he won dozens of titles, while traveling an estimated 250,000 miles by dog team.

And the All-Alaska Sweepstakes? The race series was never revived after the war, but its place in history was assured. The Sweepstakes had laid the foundation for a sport that would, as Albert Fink had predicted, become a favorite throughout Alaska. Ultimately, the race would serve as an inspiration for another mushing extravaganza to Nome, the Iditarod Trail Sled Dog Race.

The All-Alaska Sweepstakes

The Race for Life

THE 1920s MARKED the end of an epoch along the Iditarod Trail and elsewhere in Alaska's Interior. Airplanes were gradually replacing sled dog teams as the primary means of transportation, freight hauling, and mail delivery to bush communities. Yet even as their lifestyle slowly headed for extinction, a group of mushers and dogs demonstrated their value while participating in the most highly publicized and important sled dog race in Alaska's history.

No sporting event, this race was the famed diphtheria serum run of 1925, also widely known as the "Great Race of Mercy to Nome." Twenty drivers and more than 100 dogs were recruited for this run. Their mission: to relay a 20-pound package of diphtheria antitoxin serum from Nenana to Nome, where an outbreak of the disease threatened to become a fatal epidemic endangering the lives of hundreds or maybe even thousands of Alaskans. In all,

Left: *A musher arrives in Ruby, one of the relay stops during the 1925 serum run to Nome.*
Above: *The legendary Leonhard Seppala.*

the teams would travel nearly 700 miles, across one of the world's roughest and most desolate landscapes, in the depths of winter. Roughly two-thirds of their route would follow the Iditarod Trail.

The highly contagious disease that prompted this unique mission of mercy struck Nome with no forewarning. The first victims were two young Eskimo children, who died in mid-January of 1925. Dr. Curtis Welch, Nome's only physician, diagnosed the cause of their deaths as diphtheria, commonly known as the "black death." Welch knew that only a miracle could save Nome—and perhaps the entire region—from decimation. His meager supply of five-year-old antitoxin would run out after a few inoculations, if it hadn't already lost its effectiveness. Then what? With no serum, the disease would likely spread like wildfire. Natives in Nome and nearby villages would be especially vulnerable, since they'd built up no immunity to this "white man's disease."

From rails to trails: A dog team driven by "Wild Bill" Shannon prepares to begin the relay run from Nenana to Nome, following the arrival of the train that transported the diphtheria serum from Anchorage to Nenana.

Welch set up a meeting with Mayor George Maynard and the Nome City Council to request a quarantine and figure a way to get serum as quickly as possible. Maynard suggested the medicine be flown to Nome, but others balked at such a plan. In 1925, bush flying was still in its infancy. The Territory's few planes had open cockpits and had been used only in summer. No one knew if a plane could operate at minus 40 degrees Fahrenheit (or colder), or whether a pilot could keep from freezing in such conditions. And if a plane crashed, or was forced to land short of its destination, the serum would be lost. The mayor and city council finally settled on a slower, but more reliable solution: the serum would be transported via train to Nenana, where the state's rail line ended, then to Nome by dog team.

Pleas for medical assistance were quickly sent via radiotelegraph to other Alaskan communities. The nearest antitoxin supply was in

The Race for Life

Anchorage, where Dr. J. B. Beeson had 300,000 units of the lifesaving serum. If sent to Nome quickly this amount might be able to hold back the infection until a supply of one million units arrived from Seattle.

Agreeing that dog teams, not planes, offered the best hope, Alaska Governor Scott Bone ordered a relay to be organized. Mushers would travel to designated mail shelter cabins and wait their turn to transport the precious serum.

As dog drivers quickly prepared for their roles, Dr. Beeson packaged the antitoxin for shipment to Nenana by rail. The serum was placed in a cylindrical container, then wrapped in insulating material. Beeson sent the 20-pound bundle on its 298-mile train journey on January 26.

Back in Nome, meanwhile, Leonhard Seppala was gearing up for the most challenging race of his life. When it became apparent that dog teams would be used to transport the antitoxin, Nome's Board of Health had requested the services of Seppala and his legendary Siberian huskies.

Instructed to retrieve the serum at Nulato, about halfway between Nome and Nenana, Seppala chose 20 dogs for the 640-mile round-trip journey. He planned to drop 12 of them at stops along the way, so that on the return trip he could substitute fresh dogs for tired or injured ones. Using that approach, Seppala figured he could run the team both day and night.

Leading the team would be Seppala's pride and joy, a 48-pound Siberian husky named Togo. Now 12 years old, the light–gray dog with pale blue eyes had led Seppala to victories in all of Alaska's most prestigious races, including the All-Alaska Sweepstakes. One who didn't make the team was a big, black husky named Balto. Though he'd proved to be a good enough freight dog, Balto was too slow for racing. Yet he would eventually play a major—and controversial—role in the mercy mission.

On January 28, Seppala received notice that the dog team relay had begun. Unfortunately, the message failed to explain that territorial officials had decided to speed up the serum run by using a large number of relay teams over short distances. Seppala left Nome believing he would have to travel all the way to Nulato, when in fact his journey would be much shorter.

The relay began shortly before midnight on January 27, when train conductor Frank Knight passed the serum to "Wild Bill" Shannon, a former Army blacksmith who was now a mail driver. Driving a team of nine malamutes in minus-50-degree weather, Shannon drove his team to Tolovana. There he was greeted by Edgar Kalland, an Athapaskan who worked as a steamboat operator in summer and part-time mail carrier in

winter. The two men took their package into the roadhouse and warmed it by the fire, per Beeson's instructions. Then Kalland pointed his seven-dog team toward Manley Hot Springs, 31 miles away.

Fifty-five years later Kalland recalled, "It was 56 below, but I didn't notice it. We were dressed warm. We didn't have down, but I had a parky. It went below my knees, so the heat couldn't get out. You was always running or moving; your feet never got cold. . . . But then what the heck? What do you notice when you're 20 years old? You don't notice a thing. I think about it now. How did I survive?"

And so the serum was transported from one outpost to another. Mushers and dogs traveled day and night in constant subzero temperatures, through often fierce winds and occasional whiteouts. The first 15 drivers took turns carrying the serum across the Interior and finally to the village of Unalakleet, along the Bering Sea coast. They covered 465 miles

Leonhard Seppala, who carried the serum from Shaktoolik to Golovin, is shown here more than two decades later, driving a dog team through Fairbanks.

A musher drives his team through the Yukon River town of Ruby during the 1925 serum run.

in 75 hours. But more than 200 miles still remained, and reports out of Nome indicated the diphtheria was spreading rapidly.

From Unalakleet, the trail followed the coast, often battered by fierce winds and intense storms that produced whiteout conditions. Occasionally mushers would cut across the frozen sea, but at great risk. Open channels of water would appear unexpectedly, and when a strong wind blew from shore, the ice would sometimes break up and move out to sea. Rather than risk a Bering Sea shortcut, dog driver Myles Gonangnan stayed on land. Traveling through the hills between Unalakleet and Shaktoolik, his team of eight dogs was slowed by deep new snow and winds "blowing so hard that eddies of drifting, swirling snow passing between the dogs' legs and under their bellies made them appear to be fording a fast-running river."

At Shaktoolik, Gonangnan transferred the serum to Henry Ivanoff. Less than a mile out of the Eskimo village, Ivanoff's team tried to leave the trail, after picking up the scent of reindeer. He drove his sled brake into the snow to halt the half-crazed dogs, but as the sled slowed they began to fight. While trying to restore order, he saw a team approaching from the north. It was Seppala. Still unaware of the revised relay plans, the Norwegian drove his Siberians past Ivanoff's snarled team, but fortunately

Iditarod: The Great Race to Nome

heard the other musher call, "Serum—turn back!"

Though Ivanoff's team was much fresher, there was no question which musher and dog team were more qualified to make the 91-mile trip to Golovin, the next relay point. After a brief discussion, Ivanoff handed the serum and warming instructions to Seppala, who had already driven his team 170 miles over the past three days.

Turning his team around, Seppala was soon faced with a potentially life-threatening decision: should he cut across Norton Bay? The inland route was much safer, but would add several hours to the journey. And time was at a premium. After a few moments of indecision, Seppala chose the shortcut.

Forced to rely entirely on Togo's uncanny sense of direction the team headed across the ice-covered bay. Large stretches had been blasted free of snow, creating glare ice on which the dogs often slipped and fell, and the sled was constantly pushed sideways by the persistent wind. Once more, Seppala's faith in Togo was justified, as the husky unerringly led the team across the sea ice despite the darkness and blinding storm.

Upon reaching Isaac's Point, Seppala fed his dogs a large ration of salmon and seal blubber, then napped for a few hours in an igloo, with the serum placed near the fire. The team resumed its journey early the next morning, though the blizzard had worsened. Gale-force winds produced wind-chill temperatures approaching minus 100 degrees. Pushing on through the storm, his dogs completed their remarkable 260-mile journey, finally collapsing in exhaustion when they reached Dexter's Roadhouse, 78 miles from Nome.

A grizzled sourdough named Charlie Olson took the serum from Seppala and, after the ritual warming, headed into the blizzard shortly after 3:00 P.M. on January 31. Approaching Golovin Lagoon, Olson's team was blasted by strong gusts that lifted musher, dogs, and sled and hurled them off the trail. Fortunately all landed in a snowdrift and were unharmed. A short while later, Olson noticed his team slowing, which could only mean one thing: the dogs were beginning to freeze in the groin—an area not protected by thick fur. Olson stopped, and with aching, ungloved hands he carefully and methodically blanketed each dog in the team—a heroic effort that resulted in several frostbitten fingers. Now fighting for survival, the team struggled on to Bluff. Waiting there was Gunnar Kaasen, a Norwegian who'd driven teams for 21 years in Alaska. The long-time Nome resident had put together a 13-dog team for the relay. For a leader, he'd chosen Balto, the husky that Seppala had earlier rejected.

Initially the team made good time, but five miles from Bluff the dogs sank up to their bellies in drifted snow. Kaasen tried to break trail but was soon swallowed in chest-deep powder. The team had no choice but to circle around the drift. Slowly, led by Balto, it probed through the darkness and eventually regained the trail. Shortly after, while crossing the frozen Topkok River, Balto suddenly stopped and refused to move despite Kaasen's impatient shouts. The driver walked forward and was shocked to see Balto standing in a shallow overflow. Fortunately the dog had stopped in time to keep his teammates from entering the icy water.

After drying Balto's feet, the musher circled around the overflow and again pushed ahead. At one point the blowing snow became so dense that Kaasen couldn't see even those dogs closest to the sled. He had no choice but to trust Balto's instincts. The poor visibility caused Kaasen to miss the small settlement of Solomon. Instead he drove on to Bonanza Flats, where a sudden gust flipped the sled and knocked over several dogs. After righting the sled and untangling the team, Kaasen checked to see that the serum was still securely tied down. But the package was gone.

It was too dark to see. Falling to his knees, he pulled off his mittens and groped frantically through the snow with bare hands. Panicked thoughts ran through his mind. Could he have lost the serum farther back on the trail? After the serum had traveled so far, would he be the one to fail? Despair gave way to relief, however, when Kaasen's right hand touched the familiar package. After joyfully lifting it from the snow, he carefully retied it to the sled.

Kaasen's team reached Point Safety sometime after 2:00 A.M. on February 2. Inside the cabin slept Ed Rohn, who wasn't expecting Kaasen until morning. Rohn had been asked to make the final sprint to Nome, but Kaasen decided not to wake his replacement. After all, the worst was over and only 25 miles remained. And though his dogs had suffered, they were still running well. So Kaasen continued on to Nome, finally reaching the town's deserted Front Street at 5:30 A.M. The twenty teams that participated in the "great race of mercy" had traveled 674 miles through often stormy weather in less than five and a half days, a remarkable accomplishment.

Kaasen quickly ran to Welch's home and presented his package to the doctor. Using the antitoxin judiciously, Welch was able to cure those who were ill and prevent the infection from spreading. No further deaths from diphtheria were reported. The epidemic was halted and in less than three weeks the quarantine was lifted. Five days after Kaasen made his special delivery, the second batch of serum arrived in Seward. This supply was also sent by train to Nenana and then carried across the state by dog teams,

A dog team rests outside Dexter's Roadhouse in Golovin, where Leonhard Seppala passed the serum to Charlie Olson.

including many that had joined in the first relay.

After the serum run, all recognized participants were given a "donation" from a public fund, as well as per diem paid by the Territory. Most earned $30 to $40. Governor Bone also presented the drivers with a citation praising their heroism. And the H. K. Mulford Company, which produced the serum, sent inscribed medals to members of the first relay and also awarded Kaasen $1,000 for his part in the race.

Though the medical emergency ended within a few weeks, some secondary effects of the mercy mission reverberated for years afterward. On the positive side, Nome's diphtheria outbreak and the heroic serum run helped focus attention on the disease. Until 1925, diphtheria annually caused 20,000 deaths within the United States. But publicity given to the Nome epidemic helped bring about widespread inoculations and greatly reduced the disease's deadly impact.

On the down side, the serum run created considerable controversy and jealousy. In particular, Gunnar Kaasen's decision to bypass Ed Rohn started a feud that lasted several decades. Many Nome residents—Rohn and Seppala among them—claimed that Kaasen purposely bypassed Rohn to reap the publicity and other rewards given to the team that delivered the serum to Nome. Kaasen's supporters, meanwhile, accepted his explanation of the final night's events. Some even argued that it would have been a mistake to give the serum to Rohn, who had no experience traveling in stormy weather. The $1,000 reward given to Kaasen added to the controversy, as did an acting offer made to him by a motion picture company.

Seppala was further disgruntled when the media chose Balto as the serum run's canine hero and became outraged when Togo's race record was incorrectly attributed to the big freighting dog. But the final, crushing blow came when Balto, instead of Togo, was immortalized in a cast–bronze statue that was placed in New York City's Central Park.

Perhaps, as Seppala insisted, greater credit should have been given to Togo. But the statue of Balto seems a fitting tribute to an ordinary husky who came through against heavy odds, and was a representative of all canine participants in the great serum race, who were truly man's best friends in the winter of 1925.

A view of Nome in 1902, showing the tent city that was built up along the Bering Sea coast.

The Serum Mushers, 1925

Relay Sequence

"Wild Bill" Shannon	Nenana to Tolovana	52 miles
Edgar Kalland	Tolovana to Manley Hot Springs	31 miles
Dan Green	Manley Hot Springs to Fish Lake	28 miles
Johnny Folger	Fish Lake to Tanana	26 miles
Sam Joseph	Tanana to Kallands	34 miles
Titus Nikolai	Kallands to Nine Mile Cabin	24 miles
Dave Corning	Nine Mile Cabin to Kokrines	30 miles
Harry Pitka	Kokrines to Ruby	30 miles
Billy McCarty	Ruby to Whiskey Creek	28 miles
Edgar Nollner	Whiskey Creek to Galena	24 miles
George Nollner	Galena to Bishop Mountain	18 miles
Charlie Evans	Bishop Mountain to Nulato	30 miles
Tommy Patsy	Nulato to Kaltag	36 miles
Jackscrew	Kaltag to Old Woman Shelter	40 miles
Victor Anagick	Old Woman Shelter to Unalakleet	34 miles
Myles Gonangnan	Unalakleet to Shaktoolik	40 miles
Henry Ivanoff	Starts from Shaktoolik, hands to Seppala	
Leonhard Seppala	Shaktoolik to Golovin	91 miles
Charlie Olson	Golovin to Bluff	25 miles
Gunnar Kaasen	Bluff to Nome	53 miles
	Total	674 miles

The Race for Life

Jerry Austin's 20-dog team crosses a small lake near the Finger Lake checkpoint during the 1991 Iditarod. The Alaska Range looms in the background.

Iditarod: The Great Race

Origins of the Iditarod Race

THE YEAR WAS 1966. Four decades had passed since airplanes had begun to edge out sled dog teams as the mail carrier of choice. Now even more drastic changes were occurring. Sled dog racing had continued to survive—and even thrive—in some population centers, most notably Fairbanks and Anchorage. But throughout much of Alaska, mushing was on the downslide; the sled dog sub-culture seemed headed for extinction. The decline was most evident in small rural communities, where sled dogs were rapidly being replaced by snowmobiles.

"Dog teams were disappearing fast in the mid-1960s," recalls Joe Redington, Sr., a transplanted Oklahoman who came to Alaska in 1948. "Snowmachines were taking over in the villages. When I visited Interior villages in the fifties, every household had five or six dogs. They were the only transportation. But by the

---

Left: *Sled dogs belonging to Jacques Philip's*
1987 team rest during the warmth of the day.
Above: *Joe Redington, Sr.*

late 1960s, village dogs were almost gone."

Redington, a devoted musher, didn't like that disappearing act. But neither did he have a solution—at least not until he met Dorothy Page at the 1966 Willow Winter Carnival. Then and there, the future "Mother and Father of the Iditarod" had a conversation that helped revive and reenergize the sport of mushing in Alaska.

Page, a self-described history buff, had seen her first sled dog race in 1960, shortly after moving to Alaska from California. In 1966, she'd been named president of the Wasilla–Knik Centennial Committee; her primary task was to organize an event to celebrate the 100th anniversary of America's purchase of Alaska from Russia. She decided to stage "a spectacular dog race to wake Alaskans up to what mushers and their dogs had done for Alaska. We wanted to pay them a tribute."

The Iditarod Trail seemed ideal for such an event. It was, after all, a famous route used by mushers during the gold rush era. And it passed through both Knik and Wasilla, which would bring the race close to home. There was only one problem, but it was a big one: no dog driver would back the idea. Then Page crossed paths with Redington at the Willow carnival. Little did she know it, but Joe Sr. was the perfect man for the job.

Born February 1, 1917, "in a tent on the Chisholm Trail in Oklahoma," Redington was fathered by a drifting laborer who variously worked as a farmer, rancher, and oil-field worker. His mother was an "Oklahoma outlaw who took off for the hills" shortly after Joe's birth. Following his mother's departure, Joe shared a nomadic life with his father, James, and brother, Ray. In 1948, the family's travels brought them to Alaska. Shortly after crossing the border, the Redingtons stopped for fuel. The owners of the service station presented them with a gift: a puppy. It was, in retrospect, an omen of things to come.

The Redingtons weren't rich, but Joe used what money he had to buy land in Knik. By chance, that property was adjacent to the Iditarod Trail, which after a quarter-century of disuse had become overgrown. In fall 1948, Redington met Lee Ellexson, an Alaskan sourdough who'd driven mail-carrying dog teams along the Iditarod Trail in the early 1900s. "Lee sold me some sled dogs," Joe says. "He'd tell me stories of the old days and took me out on the trail. He sold me on mushing."

By the end of his first winter in Alaska, Redington owned 40 dogs and had started up his Knik Kennels. At first he used the dogs for work rather than recreation. They hauled equipment and the logs Redington used to build his cabins. They also helped in rescue and recovery missions. Redington contracted with the U.S. Air Force to recover the wreckage of

Dorothy Page, a self-described history buff, came up with the idea of a race along the Iditarod Trail to celebrate Alaska's centennial, thus earning the title "Mother of the Iditarod."

In the fall of 1980, Joe Redington, Sr. (left), and 1978 Iditarod champion Dick Mackey nailed the first official Iditarod Historic Trail marker to a willow tree near Redington's home in Knik.

aircraft that had crashed and to rescue, or recover the remains of, military personnel. From 1949 to 1957, using teams of 20 to 30 dogs, he hauled millions of dollars' worth of parts and hundreds of servicemen from remote areas. From 1954 to 1968, he also used dog teams in his work as a hunting guide. But always he kept a special interest in the Iditarod Trail.

In the early 1950s, Joe and his wife, Vi, began to clear portions of the trail and lobbied to have it added to the National Historic Trail System. (Congress finally designated the Iditarod a national historic trail in 1978.) Then, in 1966, Dorothy Page proposed her centennial race.

Joe Sr. excitedly responded, "That would be great." But he agreed to support Page's idea only if the event offered $25,000 in total prize money, an extraordinary amount for that time. (The prize money, or "purse," is divided among the top finishers, usually down to tenth or twentieth place.) By contrast, Anchorage's long-established Fur Rendezvous World Championship offered only $7,500 in 1967. "I wanted the biggest dog race in Alaska," he explains. "And the best way to do that was to offer the biggest purse."

The proposed event, scheduled for mid-February 1967, initially met with considerable opposition. Some of Alaska's most notable mushers

Joe Redington, Sr., keeps a daily log of his training runs while preparing for the Iditarod race. Redington's training camp is located in the Trapper Creek area, just south of the Alaska Range's foothills. The large pot on the barrel wood stove is used to melt snow for drinking water.

predicted it would fail miserably. Instead, it was a smashing success that attracted an all-star field of 58 racers. Run in two heats over a 25-mile course, the race was officially named the Iditarod Trail Seppala Memorial Race, in honor of mushing legend Leonhard Seppala.

Over the years, the Iditarod Trail Sled Dog Race's origins have been closely linked with the "great mercy race" to Nome. Most people believe the Iditarod was established to honor the drivers and dogs who carried the diphtheria serum, a notion the media have perpetuated. In reality, "Seppala was picked to represent all mushers," Page stressed. "He died in 1967 and we thought it was appropriate to name the race in his honor. But it could just as easily have been named after Scotty Allan. The race was patterned after the Sweepstakes races, not the serum run."

The centennial race was won by Isaac Okleasik, a resident of Teller on the Seward Peninsula. His portion of the purse was $7,000, by far the

Joe Redington, Sr., poses with spring puppies at his Knik Kennels. He runs one of the largest kennel operations in Alaska, and annually leases dog teams to Iditarod mushers from the Lower 48 and overseas.

biggest mushing payday of that era. But the Iditarod soon appeared to be a one-time big deal. The race was canceled in 1968 for lack of snow and interest. It was reinstated in 1969, but only $1,000 in prize money could be raised. Not surprisingly, the field also shrank, from 58 to 12 mushers.

Enthusiasm for an Iditarod Trail race all but died that year. Only one person kept the dream alive: Joe Sr. Rather than see it fade away, he wanted to expand the event, make it longer, better, more lucrative. Initially, Redington planned a race from Knik to the gold-boom ghost town of Iditarod. "Everybody asked, 'Where the hell is Iditarod?' Nobody knew anything about Iditarod then," Joe recalls. "So I changed it to Nome. Everybody knew where Nome is. That was our first smart move."

It may have been smart, but it wasn't well received. Skeptics labeled the proposed thousand-mile sled dog race an "impossible dream." And some folks began calling Redington the "Don Quixote of Alaska." Paying no attention to the cynics, Redington promised in 1969 that there would be a long-distance race to Nome by 1973, with an outrageous purse of $50,000. Despite some major obstacles, trail clearing and fund raising among them, Redington pulled off his impossible dream. Thirty-four drivers signed up for the first-ever sled dog race across Alaska and $51,000 was raised.

Joe Sr. billed the Iditarod as a 1,049-mile race (still the official distance). There was no question the course was at least 1,000 miles long; and the 49 was intended to symbolize Alaska, the forty-ninth state. In reality, the distance traveled by Iditarod teams is well over 1,100 miles.

Twenty-two of the 34 teams reached Nome in March 1973. The winner was Dick Wilmarth, a little-known entrant from the tiny community of Red Devil, who finished in 20 days. A mysterious footnote to the race involves Wilmarth's lead dog, "Hot Foot," which somehow got loose at the end of the trail in Nome and was not seen again until two weeks later, after it had found its way back home to Red Devil more than 500 miles away. His return is especially amazing because there are two major rivers, the Yukon and the Kuskokwim, between Nome and Red Devil.

The race had exceeded everyone's expectations, even Redington's. But another serious and unforeseen problem had arisen: a large number of dogs died along the trail (depending on which published account you read, the toll was 16 to 30 animals), causing an uproar and protests, especially among animal rights groups.

"We got lots of letters and telegrams telling us to stop this cruel race," Redington says. "Even Governor Bill Egan wrote to us. There was a lot of pressure to stop. The SPCA took out half-page ads. It's true a lot of dogs died, mostly from pneumonia and dehydration. It wasn't good. But we were trying to take good care of the dogs. The first two years were tough on the dogs, but gradually we learned how to properly care for them."

The next year, the Iditarod continued to have financial problems—the purse dropped to $34,000. Yet 44 mushers signed up. Carl Huntington, a racer from the Interior village of Galena, took first place in 20 days, 15 hours. Afterward, Redington took a poll of the mushers. "I asked them, 'Do you want to see another race?' They all said yes. I think it was established after 1974. The mushers said they'd go even if the purse wasn't big."

The 1975 Iditarod was a landmark race for two reasons: a major

corporate sponsor pledged $50,000, and several rules were added to ensure proper care and health of the dogs. The dog death rate dropped dramatically that year, with two reported losses. But in 1976, the race's sponsor withdrew its financial backing in response to continued negative publicity about dog care. The Iditarod Trail Committee's Board of Directors wanted to postpone the event two years while building its finances, but Redington refused, believing that such a postponement "would have killed the race."

With help from Dorothy Page and her husband, Von, Joe Sr. again kept the show going. The race has grown steadily—with a few rough episodes along the way—ever since. Now approaching its twentieth birthday, the Iditarod has earned international fame as "The Last Great Race on Earth."

The race purse has increased to $300,000, with $50,000 awarded to the champion. It has become the media event of March. Dozens of journalists from throughout the United States and overseas have reported from the

Joe Redington, Sr., is greeted by wife Vi and long-time friend David Karp in 1982, after passing under the famed burled spruce arch that marks the Iditarod's finish line in Nome. Joe Sr. finished the '82 race in seventeenth place.

Iditarod: The Great Race to Nome

A sled dog gets the rare privilege of sleeping in the sled, at the Rainy Pass checkpoint. Normally mushers nap on the sled, but on this occasion the sled became a dog bed.

natural abilities. Race rules list 10 general types of drugs drivers may not give their dogs, including stimulants, muscle relaxants, sedatives, anti-inflammatory drugs, and anabolic steroids. Race veterinarians will, if necessary, use drugs to treat an injured or sick dog, but that dog is then automatically withdrawn from the race.

No musher has ever been disqualified for dog drug abuse. But a problem over the years has been physical abuse of dogs. To ensure the well-being of dogs competing in the Iditarod, race officials have established a comprehensive set of rules governing "Dog Procedures." Among other things, these rules address:

• Dog numbers. Mushers must begin with at least seven and no more than 20 dogs, and have at least five dogs in harness at all times. No dogs may be added to teams after the race has started.

The Mushers

Who are these men and women competing in the race to Nome?

The large majority of the Iditarod's 60 to 70 entrants reside in Alaska's Southcentral, Interior, and Northwest regions and represent a broad spectrum of the state's population. Most live in rural areas, commonly known as the "bush," where they lead subsistence lifestyles. Hunting, fishing, trapping, and gardening are important parts of their lives. A few are urban dwellers, living in or near the Anchorage metropolis. About 10 percent are typically Outsiders from the Lower 48, Canada, or overseas.

Only a handful of entrants would be classed as professional mushers, who earn a living as sled dog racers—Susan Butcher, Rick Swenson, Joe Redington, Sr., and Joe Runyan are prime examples. These are the large-kennel owners, with 100 to 200 dogs, devoting themselves to the sport year-round.

For most Iditarod mushers, sled dog racing is either a part-time business or a hobby, albeit an expensive one. Race-related costs range from $10,000 to more than $25,000, including the $1,249 entry fee plus dog food, equipment, kennel maintenance, dog-care expenses, transportation, and training. And except for the highest finishers, financial rewards are lean. The 1991 Iditarod had a purse of $300,000, with a winner's share of $50,000. But only the top 10 places paid more than $10,000.

Iditarod mushers represent a wide array of professions and ages. Many work seasonal jobs to support their "habit." The race lineup has included carpenters, commercial fishermen, hunting guides, lawyers, surgeons, veterinarians, airline pilots, reindeer herders, gold miners, plumbers, personnel managers, small-business owners, writers, biologists, ivory carvers, corporate presidents, members of the military, and retired persons.

Whatever the size of their kennels or the nature of their goals, Iditarod racers typically begin training in late summer or early fall. Four-wheelers, motorized carts, or trucks are used to run the dogs when no snow is available, and heavy-duty preparation begins once the ground is covered in white. From November through March, everything takes a back seat to mushing concerns, as dog owners prepare their teams for the grueling trek to Nome with ever-longer training runs. By race day, most will have traveled 2,000 miles or more with their teams.

Musher Glenn Findlay, at 40 degrees below 0 during the 1982 race.

Dee Dee Jonrowe shows signs of exhaustion at Eagle Island, in 1991.

Blackie, owned by Joe Redington, Sr., has a frosty look after rubbing his head in snow upon the team's arrival at McGrath.

- Shipping dropped dogs. Mushers may leave dogs at designated dog-drop sites. (Dogs may be dropped at all but three of the Iditarod's 26 checkpoints; they're shipped to a holding center for later pickup.)
- Dog care. The chief veterinarian may penalize any musher if proper care is not maintained.
- Hauling dogs. Mushers may not allow any dogs to be hauled by another team. If dogs must be carried in the sled (because of injury, illness, or exhaustion, for example), they must be hauled in a humane fashion and covered if conditions require.
- Cruel or inhumane treatment of dogs. Mushers aren't allowed to commit "any action or inaction that causes preventable pain or suffering" (Rule 30).

Mushers found guilty of cruel or inhumane treatment may be disqualified from the race. From 1973 through 1991, at least five mushers were kicked out of Iditarod races because they violated Rule 30 and one was permanently barred because race officials felt he showed a pattern of dog abuse over several years.

Iditarod officials admit that race disqualifications—and in the extreme, lifetime banishment—are intended to send a message, both to mushers and to the public. As race marshal Donna Gentry explained after the expulsion of a musher in 1985, "This problem does not reflect the race as a whole. Mushers as a group take care of their dogs at the sacrifice of themselves. There is a special bond that develops between a musher and his dogs. They become part of the family."

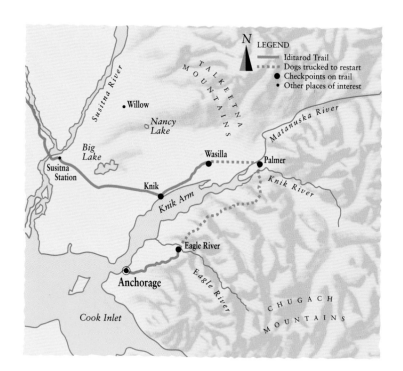

Anchorage to Wasilla

RACE DAY, 7:00 A.M. Most of Anchorage still sleeps as dawn breaks over the Chugach Mountains. But Fourth Avenue, which normally resembles a ghost town on weekend mornings, buzzes with activity.

The official start of the Iditarod Trail Sled Dog Race, traditionally staged on the first Saturday in March, is two hours away. A crowd of mushers, dog handlers, veterinarians, race organizers, media representatives, and bleary-eyed spectators has already gathered in downtown Anchorage. Dozens of dogs have been unloaded from the trucks that brought them to the staging area (they travel in compartmented camperlike shells called "dog boxes"), and the canine heroes of this sporting drama serenade the city with a symphony of barks, yips, yaps, and howls.

The Fourth Avenue staging area stretches five city blocks.

Left: *Rick Swenson reaches out to wife Kathy while leaving the downtown Anchorage starting chute in 1985.*
Above: *The race route from Anchorage to Wasilla.*

Sled dogs belonging to Joe Garnie's team wait in their dog box compartments before the Iditarod start.

Many of the mushers are already busy checking their gear and packing it into sleds. Race officials move among the dogs, marking each and every one with a dab of paint for identification purposes. Drivers are not allowed to add any dogs after the race begins and the markings are intended to prevent illegal substitutions.

Most mushers have been awake for hours. Some haven't slept all night, victims of high anxiety. Veterans as well as rookies are affected by pre-race butterflies. "There's always some jitters, no matter how many times you go through this," admits Joe Garnie, who's competed in nine Iditarods and finished second to Susan Butcher in 1986. "Once the word is 'Go!' and you're heading down the trail, you can relax. But not before."

There are notable exceptions, of course. Butcher and Rick Swenson, the only mushers who have won more than one Iditarod crown, are the epitome of cool under pressure, seemingly impervious to race-day nerves.

"My first year [1978], I was so excited and worried about everything it was all a blur," Butcher recalls. "I can hardly remember anything that happened on race day that year. But that changed as I gained experience. Now I feel completely ready. I'm relaxed, but I still pay attention to details. You can't get lackadaisical. You still have to stay on your toes."

Like Butcher, Swenson seems calm. "I'm fine, but my crew is a little nervous," he says. "I change my helpers from time to time, so they haven't

Musher Beverly Masek and her handler/husband Jan slow the team as they head down infamous "Cordova Hill," less than a mile from the starting line in Anchorage. Thousands of spectators line the city's streets to watch the annual downtown start.

Anchorage to Wasilla

been through this as much as me. There's really nothing that worries me in this race. I know what to expect. I'm pretty relaxed."

Later, when reflecting on his first race to Nome in 1976, Swenson comments, "My biggest concern as a rookie was making it to Nome. That's still number one. You never know what's going to happen along the way."

The journey from Anchorage to Nome presents every imaginable winter challenge. In any given year, Iditarod mushers and their teams may have to endure extreme cold, waist-deep snow, hurricane-force winds, whiteouts, river overflow, moose attacks, dog fights, exhaustion, and hallucinations while crossing more than 1,000 miles of Alaska's backcountry. Yet for many racers, the scariest part of the entire journey is the trip out of Anchorage, especially since the start was moved from Mulcahy Park to the city's downtown streets in 1983.

"My biggest fear is driving my team through Anchorage," Dee Dee Jonrowe said in 1989, her seventh Iditarod. "I'll feel a lot more comfortable when I'm away from all this confusion." No one is entirely immune to such fears. Even Butcher has admitted, "I hate this part of the race, all the hubbub of getting out of town."

From the Fourth Avenue starting line, mushers must drive their teams along several miles of streets and inner-city trails before reaching the comparative safety of the foothills east of Anchorage. (Snow that's been stockpiled throughout the winter is trucked in to downtown Anchorage and spread on the roads the night before the start.) The route then roughly parallels the Glenn Highway to checkpoint 2, located in the town of Eagle River, population about 25,000.

A musher takes water from a hole chopped in the frozen Skwentna River.

In driving their teams to Nome, mushers keep to a well-planned schedule. Most run their dogs two to four hours, then rest the team. Over the long haul, teams average one to one and a half hours of rest for every hour of travel.

Carefully figured into their travel schedules are stops at each of the Iditarod's 26 official checkpoints, where mushers are required to sign in and have several items of mandatory gear inspected. Race rules require that mushers carry:

- an ax that has a handle at least 22 inches long and a head weighing at least 1¾ pounds.
- a cold-weather sleeping bag, weighing a minimum of five pounds, or

with a manufacturer's rating of 25 degrees or lower.

- a pair of snowshoes with bindings, each shoe at least 33 inches long and eight inches wide.
- eight booties for each dog, either on the dogs' feet or carried in the sled.
- promotional material provided by the race committee.

Drivers are also required to carry a minimum of two pounds of food per dog, when leaving a checkpoint, as well as one day's ration of food for themselves. Mushers don't always feed themselves the most nutritional food, but rarely will they skimp on their dogs' dietary needs. Iditarod dogs may burn up to 10,000 calories per day, so the wise racer feeds them high-energy foods. Traditional dry dog food doesn't do the job, so mushers usually supplement commercial mixes with meats such as lamb, chicken, beef, fish, liver, seal, or beaver, as well as eggs and various types of

Volunteer checker Woody Johnson (right) bundles dropped dogs in burlap bags before putting them into an "Iditarod Air Force" plane at the Rohn checkpoint. Some pilots prefer to carry dogs this way to minimize their movement during flight.

Anchorage to Wasilla

Lavon Barve puts a fleece bootie on one of his dogs before leaving the McGrath checkpoint.

Iditarod: The Great Race to Nome

vegetable oils. In recent years, several mushers have also used a fat-rich dry-food concentrate. While racing, dogs usually are fed two or three main meals per day, as well as several snacks. One of the most popular Iditarod snack foods is "honeyballs" (made of lean beef, honey, powdered eggs, brewer's yeast, vegetable oil, bonemeal, and multivitamins): the size of a baseball, they weigh about a pound, have a high calorie content, and are easy to digest.

While the need for extra food and survival gear is clear, dog booties can be just as critical to a team's well-being, particularly where the trail is hard and icy. Intended to protect dogs' feet from cuts and abrasions, booties are usually made from synthetics such as polypropylene or fleece because those materials are flexible, breathable, and dry quickly. Pulled over the dogs' feet, they are fastened with velcro straps.

The process of booting dogs is usually one of the mushers' least favorite tasks. Hands bundled in mittens or thick gloves don't have nearly enough dexterity, so it usually becomes a job for bare hands, which can be tedious and often painful, particularly when temperatures fall into the minus range.

Because they're made of soft material, booties don't last long. They are chewed apart, fall off, or simply wear out, after many miles of trail pounding. During the Iditarod, a driver may go through 1,000 booties. At

Anchorage to Wasilla

Susan Butcher (left) and Dee Dee Jonrowe share a couch during a short nap in the Ophir cabin of Dick and Audra Forsgren during the 1990 race. The mushers get very little sleep during the race; this nap lasted less than 30 minutes.

a cost of about 50 cents per bootie, that's a sizable investment. Despite the aggravations and the cost, most mushers take the time to properly boot their dogs when conditions call for it. Bill Chisolm, a veteran dog driver from Two Rivers, Alaska, explains: "Twenty minutes here, 20 minutes there, it eats you up. But for what those dogs do for us, day in and day out, it's a delight [to care for their feet]. All my dogs are my buddies. They kind of like it when I put their shoes on."

An unusual piece of mandatory gear is the promotional material, also known as the "official Iditarod cachet." A small package weighing up to five pounds, the cachet is filled with envelopes to be postmarked in both Anchorage and Nome. It is intended to symbolize the mail that mushers delivered along the Iditarod Trail during the early 1900s and has been a race tradition since 1974. At the post-race banquet, envelopes delivered by top finishers are auctioned off to raise money for the race.

The mandatory gear is just a small portion of what mushers carry on the sleds. Other necessities include stove and fuel, extra clothing and boots, headlamp and batteries, first-aid kits, and repair equipment—just about anything you'd take on a 10-day to two-week winter camping trip, with the notable exception of a tent. Most mushers simply curl up inside their sled bags to sleep, though some carry a bivy sack.

Packing the sled is a difficult balancing act, one that becomes considerably easier with experience. The key is to go as light as possible, without scrimping on critical items. Every pound of unused gear will needlessly add to the dogs' burden. On the other hand, too much "weight shaving" can lead to disaster. For the 1990 race, Lesley Ann Monk made a dubious packing decision: she left the starting line with only one pair of boots, which weren't waterproof. Less than 100 miles from Anchorage, Monk suffered the consequences. Caught in overflow, she soaked her boots. Frustrated and humbled, rather than risk frostbite she dropped out of the race.

Not everything is hauled by sled. Prior to the race, food is flown to checkpoints. Many mushers will also ship out extra booties, headlamps, batteries, tools, and sled parts. Some will even have extra sleds waiting at strategic sites; for instance, a fast, lightweight model may be delivered to Unalakleet for the final 270-mile dash to Nome.

Once mushers have signed in at a checkpoint, they follow a predictable routine: find a spot to park the dogs—preferably an out-of-the-way location where disturbances are minimal. Then haul water and start the stove (which is used to melt snow for water and cook meals). Feed the dogs, check their feet, look for any signs of injuries or illness, and bed them down. Then, if necessary, make equipment repairs. Only when such chores

Iditarod: The Great Race to Nome

IDITAROD RACE ROUTES

CHECKPOINT	DISTANCE (miles)
Anchorage to Eagle River	20
Eagle River to Wasilla	29
Wasilla to Knik	14
Knik to Skwentna	88
Skwentna to Finger Lake	45
Finger Lake to Rainy Pass	30
Rainy Pass to Rohn	48
Rohn to Nikolai	93
Nikolai to McGrath	48
McGrath to Takotna	23
Takotna to Ophir	38
Northern Route: even-numbered years	
Ophir to Cripple	60
Cripple to Sulatna Crossing	45
Sulatna Crossing to Ruby	75
Ruby to Galena	52
Galena to Nulato	52
Nulato to Kaltag	42
Southern Route: odd-numbered years	
Ophir to Iditarod	90
Iditarod to Shageluk	65
Shageluk to Anvik	25
Anvik to Grayling	18
Grayling to Eagle Island	60
Eagle Island to Kaltag	70
Kaltag to Unalakleet	90
Unalakleet to Shaktoolik	40
Shaktoolik to Koyuk	58
Koyuk to Elim	48
Elim to Golovin	28
Golovin to White Mountain	18
White Mountain to Safety	55
Safety to Nome	22
Total miles	Northern 1,161
	Southern 1,163

Iditarod entrants must pass through 26 checkpoints during their journey from Anchorage to Nome. The chart lists the checkpoints and the distances between the Iditarod official stops. Between Ophir and Kaltag the race takes two paths, to give more Interior villages a chance to serve as checkpoints. In even-numbered years teams follow the northern route, and in odd-numbered years they travel along the southern route.

Anchorage to Wasilla

Spectators Dan and Pat Eckert watch musher Terry Seaman pass by on a sunny afternoon during day one of the 1991 race. The Eckerts, dog mushers themselves, pick this spot outside Anchorage because it's not as crowded as downtown.

are completed will most of the men and women in this race take care of their own needs.

As a rule, mushers are free to leave checkpoints whenever they choose (some prefer to make their stays as short as possible, believing that their dogs rest easier out on the trail, away from commotion at checkpoints). But there is a notable exception to that rule. Since 1975, teams have been required to take a 24-hour layover at one of the race's designated checkpoints. Race regulations state that the mandatory stop be taken "at a time most beneficial to the dogs," but when is ultimately left to the mushers. It's during the 24-hour layover that time differentials from Anchorage's staggered starts are adjusted. To make sure mushers comply with the layover rule, they're required to sign both in and out when they take their "24."

The first 20-mile stretch of trail presents an obstacle course that can test the patience and dog-handling skills of even the most experienced racers. Most Iditarod entrants live, or at least train their teams, in rural

Many mushers dread the first stretch of trail, from Anchorage to Eagle River, because of the distractions posed by noisy crowds and inner-city obstacles such as tunnels, bridges, and sharp corners. This team moves along a section of trail that follows an Anchorage bike path.

Anchorage to Wasilla

areas. Their dogs aren't used to urban environments.

On race day, literally thousands of yelling, applauding, whistling spectators line Anchorage's streets, including many who come armed with cameras. Almost inevitably, despite warnings from race officials, some will also bring the family pet. The combination of huge crowds, loud noises, exploding camera-flash units, and animals running loose is enough to distract even the most disciplined dog teams. There are also street intersections to negotiate (traffic is stopped whenever dog teams approach), tunnels to pass through, bridges to cross, sharp corners to turn.

To guard against these hazards, many mushers include a city-wise dog in their team, one that can lead them safely out of town. Still, every year several drivers are forced to make unscheduled stops when their dogs refuse to follow the designated trail. Sometimes they simply stop running. Or become tangled. Or they may choose to run into, or over, the densely packed crowds. In 1983, race veteran Terry Adkins of Montana missed a turn and his team mowed down several spectators who refused to yield the right of way. "I asked them three times, politely, to move out of the way," he later explained. "Finally we just went right through and cleaned them out." Fortunately, no people or dogs were injured.

Although tangles, sit-down strikes, and unplanned detours are the usual problems mushers face when leaving Anchorage, some mushers have suffered serious crashes while driving through the urban jungle.

In 1979, Gayle Nienhueser was dumped from his sled when it hit a pile of snow less than a mile from the starting line. Nienhueser felt a sharp pain in his left arm as he hit the ground, but he wasn't about to end his dream so quickly. The Anchorage musher resumed his journey despite an arm that "hurt bad for two days." Eventually the pain subsided, but "you sorta could hear a crunch, crunch," he reported. Finally, at Rainy Pass—about 225 miles from Anchorage—Nienhueser had a veterinarian look at the injured arm. On the doctor's advice, he flew back to Anchorage, where X rays showed a severe sprain. Wearing a half-cast, Nienhueser returned to his waiting team and finished the race in slightly more than 22 days.

The Anchorage–to–Eagle River stretch took an even greater toll in 1985, when three sleds crashed into a boulder while rounding a sharp curve in the trail. No dogs were injured, but all three mushers got hurt. Italian entrant Armen Khatchikian was knocked to the ground and injured his shoulder so severely that he had to scratch from the race. Norman Vaughan of Anchorage hurt his knee at the same site, and though he tried to continue, the Iditarod's oldest competitor (he was 80 at the time) was forced to drop out at Rabbit Lake, about 115 trail miles from Anchorage.

Because of deep snow, this moose refused to leave the trail, forcing mushers to snowshoe a detour around the animal.

The third victim was Joe Redington, Sr., who was hurled into a tree. Redington injured his right arm, but refused to call it quits. "I guess I'm getting used to being banged up," said Joe Sr., then 68 years old. "Been banged up so many times I've come to expect it. If it had been my left arm, it wouldn't have been so bad. Never could use my left arm. But I guess I'll learn now."

For mushers, there's a painful irony to the trauma associated with the start of the race: Anchorage wasn't part of the original Iditarod Trail system. From a historical perspective, the port city of Seward would be a more appropriate starting point. But logistically and financially Anchorage makes better sense. With a population of about 226,000, Anchorage is the state's population, communications, and business center. And it is, after all, only 20 miles or so from the historic Seward-to-Nome route. What better place is there to focus attention on Alaska's "Last Great Race"?

Malcolm Vance balances himself on his sled's handlebars, to avoid a stretch of open water along the trail between Anchorage and Eagle River. Unseasonably warm weather at the start of the 1991 race made the trail sloppy in many areas.

Anchorage to Wasilla

Above: *Aerial view, showing Joe Redington, Sr.'s, arrival at Eagle River; from there, teams are trucked to the Wasilla restart.*
Opposite: *A musher travels through the Moose Run Golf Course at Fort Richardson, outside Anchorage.*

"I'm not sure what [mushers] have to complain about," says Swenson. "Where else are we going to get this level of attention? The race needs this exposure. And mushers need this exposure. The public knows [the Anchorage start] is bogus. But it's really the only time that most of these people can see us. It's all part of the race, ceremonial or whatever."

By 8:30 A.M., Fourth Avenue is bedlam. Hundreds of dogs are now placed in harness and they howl in anticipation of the run ahead. Media types scurry for last-minute interviews, while mushers recheck their gear, pose for pictures, politely sign autographs, and give out orders to handlers. The race announcer tells spectators over a PA system that they must now leave the staging area and stand behind the slatwood fencing placed along the street.

Shortly before 9:00, a contingent of race officials approaches the starting line, which is marked by a huge Iditarod banner and flags of Alaska, the United States, and all other countries with entrants in the race. A ceremonial ribbon cutting is followed, precisely at 9:00, by the traditional "send-off" of an honorary number–one musher. Often, this position is reserved for one of the 1925 serum run participants.

At 9:02, the race officially begins, and teams leave the starting chute at two-minute intervals until the entire field has departed. Positions were determined at a pre-race drawing, staged at a banquet two evenings earlier.

To keep their adrenaline-pumped dogs from running out of control, racers add weight to the sleds at the start. They're required to carry a passenger—a friend or family member—on the run to Eagle River to counter the team's initial surge of energy. Assuming they survive all the inner-city hazards, mushers will arrive in two to three hours. There, they'll unharness the dogs, put them back in their dog boxes, and drive about 30 highway miles to the restart site in Wasilla.

It wasn't always that way. In the first two Iditarods, teams followed a trail across upper Cook Inlet to Knik. But in years when the weather is unseasonably warm, portions of the inlet and its mudflats remain unfrozen and too hazardous for crossing. So in the mid-'70s, organizers decided it would be safest to truck the dogs to a restart site. Originally based at Knik, the site was moved in 1989 to Wasilla, home of the Iditarod's headquarters.

Here the race to Nome begins for real.

Halverson, who says he always carries a gun when traveling by dog team, fired four shots into the moose before it went down. "I was praying on that last one," he said. "I only had one bullet left."

The toll on Butcher's team was heavy. Two dogs died and six others were seriously hurt, suffering either from leg damage or internal injuries. With only eight of her 16 dogs left and several of those in questionable condition, Butcher dropped out of the race.

Except for moose, there are few extraordinary challenges along the 100-mile section of trail from Wasilla to Skwentna. The terrain is generally flat and the route—marked with painted stakes, tripods, reflectors, or flagging—is easy to follow. Usually. On at least a few occasions, frontrunning teams have lost valuable time early in the race because they somehow got onto a false trail.

In 1982, race leaders Larry "Cowboy" Smith and Herbie Nayokpuk

A pair of Peter Thomann's Siberian huskies rest in the sun at Skwentna. Though favored during the All-Alaska Sweepstakes, Siberians are no longer the race dog of choice, having been replaced by mixed-breed huskies.

Volunteers Make It Happen!

Veterinarian Stuart Nelson, right, cares for Raymie Redington's dog.

Radio ham operator Kent Reinke and checker Scott Otterbacher, at Rohn.

Mushers and dogs are the focus of attention when the Iditarod is run each March. But the race from Anchorage to Nome wouldn't be possible without the behind-the-scenes work of Iditarod volunteers. Literally thousands of Alaskans, and many men and women from outside the state as well, help to organize this mushing extravaganza:

• Snowmachine crews break trail for the racers and mark the route, often while enduring extreme cold, fierce winds, or blizzards.

• Airplane pilots, known collectively as the "Iditarod Air Force," fly dog food and other supplies into checkpoints along the route, provide transportation for race officials, and make themselves available for any necessary search-and-rescue operations.

• Veterinarians conduct pre-race examinations on the dogs, check their well-being at checkpoints along the trail, report dog-care rule infractions, and carry out any required emergency medical procedures.

• Ham radio operators stationed at checkpoints provide race updates, relay messages, and coordinate search-and-rescue operations.

• Many families in checkpoint communities open their homes to mushers and race officials, providing lodging and meals. Often, cooking is a community project.

• Designated "checkers" sign in mushers at checkpoints, make certain that mushers are carrying their mandatory gear, and provide information to racers, officials, and the media.

• Computer operators make updated race information available to the media and the public.

• Other volunteers serve as dog handlers at the Iditarod start, answer phones at race headquarters, make dog booties, look after dogs that have been dropped from the race, or simply act as all-around errand runners.

Though most volunteers keep a low profile, their contributions are not overlooked. As one race official explained, "There wouldn't be an Iditarod without the volunteers."

Pilot George Murphy handles a dropped dog.

took a wrong turn only one mile from the Skwentna checkpoint. Following a homesteader's snowmobile trail that crossed the race route, Smith and Nayokpuk traveled about 25 miles in the wrong direction before realizing their mistake. By the time they reached Skwentna, 16 mushers had already arrived. Joe Redington, Sr., Susan Butcher, and rookie Mitchell Seavey also took the wrong turn, but recognized their mistake after only a few miles. Still, Butcher complained, the detour "cost me the race right there. The dogs [which can lose their enthusiasm if forced to retrace their path] never got it back." Butcher may have been right. She finished the 1982 Iditarod in second place, only three minutes and 43 seconds behind Rick Swenson.

Race officials later reported that the trail had been sufficiently well marked. But traveling at night, the mushers had somehow missed the markings. Although the chances of getting lost are greater, most Iditarod mushers prefer to run their teams at night if possible, particularly when traveling through the "banana belt" of Southcentral Alaska. Alaskan

Above: *Jan Masek drives his team along the trail as it parallels Knik Road, with the Talkeetna Mountains in the background.*
Overleaf: *Tim Moerlein drives his dogs along Knik Flats during the 1986 race, with the Chugach Mountains rising in the distance. The trail has since been changed so it no longer passes through the flats.*

Wasilla to Rohn

Iditarod: The Great Race to Nome

but Butcher has now unquestionably usurped that title. Even Swenson once admitted, albeit in the heat of battle, "The rest of us are just in a different class."

The changing of the championship guard at least temporarily caused a rift in what was once a close friendship. During the summer of 1985, Butcher said the Susan-vs.-Rick rivalry was "all blown out of proportion by the press. Rick is just about my best friend. It's just that when we're racing, we have a hard time being around each other. We're both so competitive, we both have that drive. That makes it tough to be real buddy-buddy during the Iditarod. But afterward, we talk over the race and get it out of our systems. Then we're back to being good friends." As evidence of their friendship, Butcher even asked Swenson to be her "bridesmaid" when she married Dave Monson in 1985, and Swenson's wife, Kathy, baked the wedding cake.

Susan Butcher runs up the bank of the Yukon River upon arriving at Kaltag during the 1989 Iditarod.

Wasilla to Rohn

Joe Delia—trapper, postmaster, and Iditarod volunteer—stands outside his family's cabin at Skwentna.

But during the late 1980s, the onetime neighbors became separated by physical and emotional distance. Swenson moved from Eureka to Two Rivers, located much closer to Fairbanks, and the two bickered publicly. Some suggested that Swenson couldn't stand Butcher's success or her favored image with the public and press. Rick and Susan tended to shrug off their strained relationship, however, saying it's only natural they'd be cool to each other, given their competitive makeups.

In 1991, their relationship took another curious turn. The intensity of their rivalry was perhaps never greater, as each attempted to be the first Iditarod musher to win a fifth championship. Yet when questioned about it, Butcher commented, "We have been friends for 15 years. We are just tough competitors."

Butcher was in first place, one hour ahead of Swenson, when she made that statement at Elim. Only 101 miles from Nome, she appeared to own an insurmountable lead. But in one of the Iditarod's biggest turnabouts and most dramatic finishes ever, Butcher's team was stopped by a blinding blizzard between White Mountain and Safety, while Swenson drove his dogs through the storm and on to a record-setting fifth victory.

After her retreat to White Mountain, when it had been apparent that she couldn't catch her rival, Butcher said, "I'm very, very, very happy for

Race marshal Donna Gentry halted the race at Rainy Pass because stormy weather had prevented the Iditarod's volunteer pilots from delivering dog food to the next two checkpoints. (Mushers are required to get their food to Anchorage a couple of weeks before the Iditarod, so it can be flown to checkpoints along the trail.) Gentry decided that the absence of food at checkpoints farther up the trail, combined with poor weather and marginal trail conditions, presented a significant threat to the teams. So she held up the race until delivery was confirmed.

Iditarod frontrunners and tailenders are normally separated by more than a day's travel when they reach Rainy Pass Lodge, located along the shores of Puntilla Lake. With a steady stream of teams coming in and going out of the checkpoint, there's never more than a dozen or so present at a given time. But the race stoppage enabled back-of-the-packers to catch up to the leaders and eventually the entire field was gathered at Rainy Pass Lodge. With 58 mushers and 806 dogs waiting for a series of storms to end, it didn't take long for the mushers' food supplies to be exhausted.

A food crisis was averted, however, thanks to a couple of airborne mercy missions. While stormy weather kept Iditarod planes from flying across the Alaska Range, several Anchorage-based pilots were able to land on Puntilla Lake. First, about 3,000 pounds of dog food was delivered. Then, a surprise gift from the people of Anchorage was dropped off: in response to a plea for help issued by the Iditarod Trail Committee, the public had donated more than two tons of people food. The shipment included everything from beefsteaks to military C-rations.

As the freeze dragged on, racers expressed mixed emotions about their enforced wait. "Rainy Pass is probably the most ideal place on the trail to wait, if you have to," said Vern Halter, a mushing attorney from Moose Creek. "We've got a warm, dry place to stay [one of the lodge buildings was designated a "mushers' cabin"]. And now we have food for ourselves and the dogs. Plus the people in charge of this place [Robin and Bucky Winkley] have done just an excellent job making things comfortable for us. On the other hand, we've only gone 200 miles and it's been nearly a week. We've got almost 1,000 to go. That's kind of depressing. Everybody's antsy, but what can you do? All you can do is wait."

Finally, after three days, the dog food reached its destination and Gentry lifted the freeze, allowing mushers to resume their trek to Nome. (That same year, the second freeze in race history was ordered, at the Interior town of McGrath. Again the Iditarod was halted because storms prevented dog food delivery to checkpoints farther up the trail.)

From the lodge, teams continue their gradual ascent to the divide that

Opposite: *Dee Dee Jonrowe takes a nap at the Rainy Pass Lodge checkpoint in 1990, before continuing on through the Alaska Range.*
Above: *Dan MacEachen runs behind his team while ascending through the Rainy Pass area, as day breaks in the Alaska Range during the 1986 race.*

Ray Dronenberg and his dogs are buffeted by 15-mile-per-hour winds as they pass through the Alaska Range in 1986.

serves as gateway to the Interior. During the first four Iditarods, mushers drove their teams through Ptarmigan Pass, also known as Hell's Gate. But in 1977, the route was moved to Rainy Pass, which was part of the original Iditarod Trail. The switch has cut the run from Rainy Pass Lodge to Rohn nearly in half, from 88 to 48 miles.

Above Puntilla Lake, mushers pass beyond the tree line into alpine tundra. In winter, this is a vast, desolate world of white. Surrounded by rugged peaks rising above 5,000 feet, the teams climb a valley that offers little or no protection from wind-driven blizzards roaring through the Alaska Range. In 1974, a group of racers got caught by a severe mountain storm. Temperatures to minus 50 degrees and 50-mile-per-hour winds dropped the wind chill to minus 130. The mushers were lucky. They all survived and only a few were frostbitten. But many Iditarod veterans say it's only a matter of time before someone isn't so fortunate.

Iditarod: The Great Race to Nome

Beverly Masek gives her team a rest break along the Tatina River, just a few miles outside the "Rohn Resort."

Joe May, an Alaskan trapper who won the 1980 Iditarod, once predicted, "Somebody's going to buy it in this race. . . . I'm surprised it hasn't happened already. You talk to any musher, and every one of them has a story to tell. Some of them have come awfully close. Awfully close."

One was Norman Vaughan of Anchorage. A retired Air Force colonel, Vaughan had plenty of mushing and cold-weather experience. In 1928, he drove a dog team in Admiral Richard Byrd's successful expedition to the South Pole. Four years later he competed in the first, and last, Winter Olympics sled dog race, at Lake Placid, New York. And during World War II he was named commander of the military's first dog team search-and-rescue unit.

Vaughan entered his first Iditarod in 1975 at age 69, but was forced to scratch. Not about to be discouraged, he tried again in '76. By the time the race had entered the Alaska Range, he was in last place, traveling alone. About seven miles beyond the lodge, a strong wind began to howl. Soon his team was stuck in a thick ground blizzard that obliterated the trail. Wading through deep snow, unable to get his bearings, Vaughan criss-crossed the valley, vainly seeking the race route. After three days of futile searching, both musher and dogs had run out of food.

"On the fourth day, the dogs had eaten my harnesses," he later reported. "I don't mean chewed them off, I mean eaten them completely. I only had five harnesses left from the 14 I started with. I was pulling the sled in snowshoes, pulling those dogs. Still the sled wouldn't move." Eventually Vaughan drove his team far off the race trail. When he failed to

Wasilla to Rohn

Left: *Claire Philip negotiates a narrow trail as her team approaches the infamous Dalzell Gorge. Caribou tracks are in the foreground.*
Above: *Francine Bennis's team skirts open water while crossing Dalzell Creek.*
Below: *The Dalzell Gorge, looking toward the Tatina River.*

arrive in Rohn, race officials launched a massive search effort using both aircraft and snowmachines, but they failed to find him for several days.

On his fifth day in the mountains, Vaughan became hypothermic: "I was thinking poorly and slowly, so I knew I'd better get in the sleeping bag because I had no other way to get warm. I had long since discarded my stove because I ran out of fuel. . . . It was then that I made the decision to kill a dog. I was going to drink the blood and feed the meat to the dogs. I thought it would be easier to do than take raw meat and swallow it."

Fortunately, no such sacrifice had to be made. Snowmachiners Gene Leonard and Frank Harvey spotted Vaughan's tracks and found him late on the fifth day. The rescuers fed Vaughan's dogs and gave him some hot coffee. Then they towed musher, dogs, and sled back to Rainy Pass Lodge.

Despite his survival ordeal, Vaughan vowed he'd be back some day to complete the race. Sure enough, he entered and completed the 1978 Iditarod, placing thirty-third (out of 34 finishers), in 22 days, three hours, 29 minutes, and 44 seconds. Through 1991, the colonel had entered 12 Iditarods, making it to Nome five times.

Extreme cold and ground blizzards are not the only hazards that teams face while driving through the Alaska Range to Rohn. Even in ideal weather, mushers can expect problems while passing through Dalzell Gorge, which more than one Iditarod musher has described as "a living nightmare." From Puntilla Lake to 3,200-foot Rainy Pass, mushers gain slightly more than 1,000 feet in elevation in about 20 miles. Once over the divide, mushers follow a steep, winding trail that plunges about 1,000 feet in five miles through a narrow, boulder-filled canyon and crosses narrow ice bridges spanning a partly frozen creek. The passage through Dalzell Gorge can be a controlled fall because dogs have difficulty getting any traction on the slippery, twisting path.

"I was scared to death," defending champion Jerry Riley admitted in 1977 after surviving a wild ride through the gorge. "It was four hours of riding my brake, trying to slow my team down—four hours of terror." Riley at least made it through the canyon with his sled and team intact— and dry. Many others have not been so lucky. In 1988, rookie driver Peryll Kyzer broke through an ice bridge and fell into the creek. After getting herself, sled, and dogs back on dry ground, she was forced to spend the night in a wet sleeping bag.

A successful passage through Dalzell Gorge doesn't always mean a musher's troubles on the way to Rohn have ended. The final length of trail follows the Tatina River and presents its own challenges. In 1986, Susan Butcher's lead dogs fell through the frozen Tatina. Her team was on glare

A team has reached the crest of Rainy Pass during the 1984 race. High winds often obliterate the trial here. Many mushers have gotten lost going through Rainy Pass because of crisscrossing trails, so most prefer to travel through this area in daylight.

ice, making it impossible to set a snow hook. But fortunately the dogs stopped, allowing Butcher the chance to run forward to where her leaders had gone through the ice. "They just disappeared," she said later. "I was terrified. I thought they'd gone completely under the water. But they were just sitting there wagging their tails. They fell about three feet onto another layer of ice." Butcher rescued the dogs, which survived the fall without injury, and finished the run into Rohn.

Those who have made the journey from Rainy Pass to Rohn more than once tend to be philosophical about that stretch of the trail. "It's like a hurdle," says Dewey Halverson. "It's just one of the big obstacles you have to get by." And Rick Swenson has noted, "What's most important is that your team is in good shape when you get to Rohn. Then you're still in the race."

Sonny Russell changes his sled runners while taking his 24-hour layover at Rohn, a favorite resting place for teams as they recover from their Alaska Range passage and prepare for their trip through the Farewell Burn.

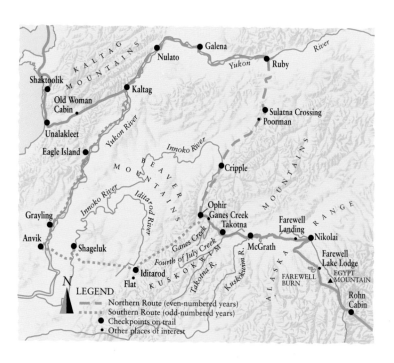

Rohn to Unalakleet

MUSHERS AND DOGS are usually ready for a lengthy rest break after their punishing dash through the Alaska Range. And there's no better place for Iditarod teams to enjoy some R&R than Rohn.

A roadhouse was built here in the early 1900s to serve the dog team drivers who hauled mail and supplies along the Iditarod Trail. The original Rohn Roadhouse is no longer standing, but in its place is a 1930s log cabin. Now owned by the federal government, the building is managed by the Bureau of Land Management as a public shelter cabin. From time to time it's also used by trappers. And for several days in early March, the cabin takes on a third role: it becomes the "Rohn Resort."

Like the original roadhouse, the resort caters to mushers and dogs while serving as Iditarod Checkpoint 8, approximately 275 miles from Anchorage as the dog team runs. The cabin offers

---

Left: *Mitch Brazen's fur ruff is crusted with ice following a nighttime run in minus 25-degree temperatures.*
Above: *The race route from Rohn to Unalakleet.*

temporary escape from the cold. It's a place to have coffee and a snack, exchange Dalzell Gorge horror stories, compare notes, or take a nap.

Just as important as the cabin is the setting. Rohn Resort is tucked in a spruce forest, near the confluence of the Tatina and Kuskokwim rivers. It's a quiet spot, protected from the wind and, for the most part, from the commotion surrounding the Last Great Race. There is no telephone (though communication is possible through a ham radio operator). And the air strip is short and rough, with a strong crosswind that makes pilots hesitant to land.

The checkpoint's remoteness greatly restricts the number of visitors—including journalists—who stop at Rohn. Thus, it's a wonderful escape for mushers and dogs, especially for the frontrunners who are under the most pressure and closest scrutiny. Which is why they often take their 24-hour layovers here.

And perhaps at no other checkpoint, with the notable exception of Nome, is an extended healing period so desirable. Not only must drivers recover from their Alaska Range ordeals, but also they must prepare physically and emotionally for the brutal 93-mile trek from Rohn to Nikolai.

For the first 45 miles out of Rohn, racers follow the Iditarod Trail along the South Fork of the Kuskokwim River. Many years, sections of the frozen river are covered by overflow, which may range from a few inches to several feet deep and can be a serious hazard.

Colonel Norman Vaughan was hospitalized with frostbitten feet in 1975 after his team ran through some overflow. "In places it was 10 inches deep and the dogs just weren't able to sustain their pace," Vaughan later explained. "I ended up leading the dogs myself and of course my feet got quite wet. The problem was, when I got past the overflow, my boots were frozen solid." The Colonel tried to cut the boots from his feet with an ax, but failed. So he drove his team 26 miles to Farewell (which has since been dropped as an Iditarod checkpoint) and caught a plane to Anchorage, where his numb, blistered feet were treated for frostbite.

The most terrifying account of the Kuskokwim's dangers was given after the 1973 race, when one team nearly fell through a huge hole in the ice. Tom Mercer, a musher from Talkeetna, compared the noisy rush of water to Niagara Falls. "I couldn't believe I was hearing it," he reported. "It was roaring up ahead, louder and louder. The ice was slick, with overflow on it, and a hole in the ice nearly 100 feet in diameter was sucking the overflow water down into the main river channel with great force."

A large, powerful man, Mercer swung his team out of the overflow current and around the gaping hole without much difficulty. But after

Checker Pat Plunkett guides Robin Jacobsen's team to a "parking spot" at Rohn during the 1991 race.

The northern lights illuminate the horizon, beyond the checker's tent at Cripple in 1986. Temperatures of minus 25 to 35 were common that year.

Vern Halter is welcomed by school children at the Yukon River village of Nulato. The Iditarod is a major event at many villages along the trail.

midway checkpoint. Yet rarely will racers push their teams to win that halfway prize. Serious title contenders aren't about to risk an early burnout for what amounts to small change. The long haul is what's important, not a midway dash for comparatively little reward. Besides, the halfway prize has come to be regarded as a jinx; only once in 19 years did the midway leader go on to win the race. Dean Osmar, a commercial fisherman from the tiny Kenai Peninsula community of Clam Gulch, was the lone exception. He surprised all the experts by capturing the 1984 crown in only his second Iditarod.

Osmar entered the race as one of many longshots. But he took the lead at Ophir, 476 miles into the race, and immediately began building a large lead. No one took him seriously. The other contenders knew Osmar's dogs weren't particularly fast. Sooner or later, they'd reel him in.

Osmar's strategy—set a fast pace early in the race, build a big lead, then hold on—wasn't anything new. The strategy had been used many times but invariably was foiled by blizzards, poor trail conditions, or dog burn-out. Larry "Cowboy" Smith, a former rodeo performer from Dawson City in Canada's Yukon Territory, was perhaps the Iditarod's best-known early pacesetter, or "rabbit." Fast starts and down-the-stretch fades became his trademark during the early 1980s. Twice he came tantalizingly close to being number one, placing fourth in 1981 and third in '83. But Cowboy was never able to keep his dogs running fast enough for long enough to finish on top.

Everyone figured that Osmar would have a similar fadeout, if not a complete crash. But he and his dogs fooled them all. Maintaining a steady, if unspectacular, pace through the Interior and then along the Bering Sea coast, he withstood a late challenge from Butcher to win by one hour and 34 minutes. Typically the rabbits are mushers who don't have the dog power to keep pace with the fastest teams if the race comes down to a final sprint along the coast. But since Osmar's unexpected win, early frontrunners aren't taken so lightly, nor are they allowed to build big leads.

For most serious contenders, the early race strategy can be summed up in two words: pacing and maintenance. As Dewey Halverson once explained, "You have to make sure the engine is running smooth, especially when you get to the coast. That's when it counts the most." The key is to stay near the front of the pack, in position to make a charge when necessary, while keeping the dog team happy and eager to run. Mushers like Swenson, Butcher, and 1989 champion Joe Runyan have become experts at that. They'll hang close until reaching the coast, then take advantage of their teams' speed to push in front where it really counts: at the end.

Checker Joe Maillelle, Sr., signs Mike Madden into Grayling during the 1991 race, while three youngsters help by bringing dog food to the musher.

In caring for their dogs, the mushers at the front of the Iditarod pack often get little sleep. Says Halverson, "If a guy is doing a good job with the dogs [and aiming for first place], there's no way you can get abundant sleep. Sometimes it's two hours, sometimes one hour, sometimes 15 minutes. But it's not enough." The Iditarod's frontrunners are usually exhausted by the time they reach the Yukon River—nearly 650 miles, and about one week's journey for the race leaders, from Anchorage. Stories of mushers falling asleep while driving their teams are not unusual.

In 1985, Halverson "fell asleep at the wheel"—and then fell off his sled. "I usually rope in, but I didn't last night," he explained. "It was one of life's embarrassing moments on the trail. I fell off and the dogs kept running." Fortunately for Halverson, Jerry Austin was following close behind and provided a ride (mushers may receive help to recover a

Joe Runyan's team negotiates an open creek between Kaltag and Unalakleet during the 1991 Iditarod. Normally dogs will run through open water without having to be coaxed, but as this sequence of photos shows, these sled dogs, perhaps tired by the 900 miles they'd already traveled, needed some extra encouragement.

Iditarod: The Great Race to Nome

Rohn to Unalakleet

Residents of Unalakleet, including tiny Ayla Ryan, greet Lavon Barve upon his team's arrival at the Bering Sea coast in 1988. Unalakeet is the largest Native community intersected by the race.

Iditarod: The Great Race to Nome

driverless team). They soon caught up with the runaway team, which had traveled about five miles before stopping. Falling off the sled is not the only hazard, however. Over the years, several mushers have received nasty injuries when they've banged into low-hanging branches while sleeping on the run.

The effects of sleep deprivation only get worse on the Yukon River, which the race trail follows for about 150 miles. Depending on the year, either Anvik or Ruby serves as "gateway" to the Yukon. Anvik is a small Athapaskan village of about 100 people, who are heavily dependent on subsistence activities such as hunting, fishing, trapping, and gardening. Ruby, meanwhile, was established during the gold rush and developed into a booming river port that served the mining camps. At its peak, Ruby's population reached 2,000 and the town served as a "cultural melting pot," filled with immigrants from several European countries.

By World War II, Ruby was on its way to becoming a ghost town like so many other gold-rush-era settlements, but was saved from extinction when a group of Natives from another village moved into the site. Ruby's current population is about 250 and most of its residents are Athapaskans who follow a subsistence lifestyle. The village's main claim to Iditarod race fame is Emmitt Peters, the "Yukon Fox."

Peters is one of three Native Alaskans to capture an Iditarod championship; the others are Carl Huntington of Galena and Jerry Riley of Nenana. Mushing a team of trapline dogs, the Yukon Fox won the 1975 race in 14 days, 14 hours, 43 minutes, and 45 seconds. For the next

A musher crosses glare ice on the Unalakleet River in 1986. That year, little snow fell along the Bering Sea coast, and much of the trail from Kaltag to Unalakleet was solid ice. The Nulato Hills are in the background.

10 years, Peters didn't miss a race. And he finished "in the money" (among the top 20) every time. In 1978, he placed third and the following year took second. His record winning time lasted five years, until Joe May broke it in 1980. Peters' string of consecutive Iditarod appearances ended in 1986, and he didn't return to the race until 1990. What he discovered was discouraging.

The Yukon Fox, so used to being a contender, had dropped into middle-of-the-pack status. He reached his hometown in thirty-seventh place and finished forty-second in the final standings. While in Ruby, he admitted it was probably the low point of his racing career. "It's kind of hard to sit back and watch the big boys get away. But I've got to face it," he said with some sadness. "I won with seven dogs, but that was back in the seventies. There's a different quality of teams now. My dogs are too big. Too slow. You've got to have greyhound dogs now. You've got to have speed."

Contrasted with Peters' subdued homecoming was Susan Butcher's arrival at Ruby. As the first musher to reach the Yukon River in 1990, she was treated to an elegant seven-course meal, courtesy of an Anchorage hotel, plus a cash prize of $2,500. Both the money and the meal are race traditions (though there have been years when neither was offered).

The Yukon passage offers a variety of obstacles, ranging from bitter cold to boredom. Temperatures may drop to minus 50 degrees and below. When combined with high winds, which mushers are almost sure to encounter somewhere along Alaska's largest river, wind-chill temperatures may fall well below minus 100 degrees. In such extreme cold, not even the dogs are enthusiastic about traveling.

The chill can be extremely demoralizing, especially when teams have difficulty following the trail, which in some years has been blown over or mismarked, along the Yukon. In 1983, racer David Monson complained that he'd lost several hours after getting off the trail. At one point he even got onto his hands and knees while searching for some sign of the route.

Long stretches of the Yukon River can become monotonous. To ease the routine, many mushers carry cassette players and/or radios. "It used to be you'd stop and have a coffee break," Rick Swenson said during the 1988 race. "Now you stop and put in a tape. I think it's important in mini-mizing mood swings and keeping you awake."

Music may help mushers stay awake, but it doesn't prevent the imagination from working overtime. Sleep deprivation often results in hallucinations along the Yukon and other sections of trail. In 1976, Eagle River racer Jon Van Zyle (who has since become the Iditarod's official artist) said: "I fell asleep, woke up, hallucinated, fell asleep, woke up—over and over again. . . . In one stretch . . . I kept seeing park benches, people playing golf, people just lolling around enjoying the sunshine, and green grass."

According to Jerry Austin, such apparitions are almost inevitable: "You push yourself so hard that after a while you just get numb. You start seeing things. I see my dogs running up into the air—up into the clouds. I see lights under the dogs' feet."

The Yukon run ends at Kaltag, an Athapaskan village of about 250 people. Here the race's northern and southern branches are joined and the trail again follows a single path. Located 800 trail miles from Anchorage and about 360 miles from Nome, Kaltag has been described as a border town—a gateway between two cultures. From there, the race trail follows a route that's been used for hundreds of years, connecting the Interior's Athapaskans with the coastal Eskimos. The teams follow this centuries-old "Kaltag Portage" for 90 miles, as it rises to a thousand-foot pass, then gradually descends toward the village of Unalakleet. When that stretch is completed, only 270 more miles remain. And the final sprint begins.

Rohn to Unalakleet

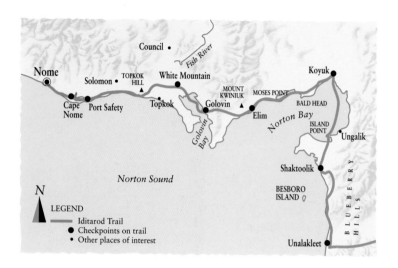

The following places are labeled on the map: Council, Fish River, Nome, Solomon, TOPKOK HILL, White Mountain, Koyuk, Cape Nome, Port Safety, Topkok, MOUNT KWINIUK, Golovin, MOSES POINT, BALD HEAD, Elim, Norton Bay, ISLAND POINT, Ungalik, Golovin Bay, Shaktoolik, Norton Sound, BESBORO ISLAND, BLUEBERRY HILLS, Unalakleet

N

LEGEND
— Iditarod Trail
● Checkpoints on trail
• Other places of interest

Unalakleet to Nome

DURING THE IDITAROD race's early years, even the most competitive mushers treated the first 800 or 900 miles as an extended camping trip. Happy to share each other's company, they traveled together, camped together, broke trail together. Until reaching the coast.

Unalakleet marked the point where camaraderie gave way to competition. As an Associated Press story reported from Unalakleet on March 20, 1977: "Now, the amiable camping trip that began March 5 in Anchorage has ended and the race is on. Leaders have dropped all but the most essential gear, and rest stops from here to the finish will be brief. Machiavellian tactics, secrets, and games are beginning as the trail moves into its final phase."

Since the early 1980s, that two-part drama has been gradually replaced by a much longer single-act play, at least for those who

---

Left: *Rick Swenson drives his team through a ground blizzard eight miles from Nome in 1988. He placed second to Susan Butcher that year.*
Above: *The race route from Unalakleet to Nome.*

At the finish line in 1991, one of Martin Buser's dogs is frosted after a chilling run from Safety. The 1991 finish was the coldest on record, with wind-chill temperatures falling to minus 62 degrees.

seek to win. As the total prize money has increased—from $50,000 in 1973 to $300,000 in 1991—the race has become increasingly competitive.

Yet even in this more competitive era, the intensity level picks up when the race leaders reach Unalakleet. The Bering Sea coast is the final proving ground, separating the elite from the also-rans. From Unalakleet on, the pace increases dramatically. As 1978 champion Dick Mackey once explained, "From here you've got to drive the dogs like they're going to cross the finish line in Nome and drop dead. They won't, of course. They're tougher than the men [or women], but that's how you've got to drive them." Mushers at this point drop all but their highest-caliber core of dogs. Most racers begin the Iditarod with 15 to 18 dogs, but few will complete their journey with more than a dozen pulling the sled.

In contrast to the mushers' growing intensity is the gaiety and spirit of celebration in Unalakleet. As in many communities along the race route, the Iditarod produces a holiday mood in this Inupiat Eskimo village. Located on the shore of Norton Sound, Unalakleet is the biggest Native settlement intersected by the Iditarod Trail. Its 800 residents support themselves largely through commercial salmon fishing and subsistence hunting and fishing. But winter is a difficult time in this windy town (Unalakleet means "place where the east wind blows"), and the Iditarod helps to brighten a somber season.

Residents keep a vigilant "Iditarod watch" as the race approaches. When teams finally come within sight of the village, their arrival is heralded by church bells or sirens. Racers are escorted into the village,

Mike Madden mushes past a church covered by a 25-foot-high snowdrift in Unalakleet. Unalakleet, the "place where the east wind blows," is known for its huge snowdrifts.

where they're swarmed by hundreds of people. Mushers are housed and fed by designated host families. Despite the gracious welcome, frontrunners usually don't stay more than a few hours—just long enough to properly rest their dogs. As soon as one musher slips out of town, others are sure to follow.

Beyond Unalakleet, the trail rises into coastal hills, then descends back toward the shoreline and the next checkpoint, Shaktoolik. In making this 40-mile run, teams are often blasted by ferocious northeast winds that whip up loose snow and create blinding ground blizzards. Inhabited by about 150 Eskimos, Shaktoolik, like most of its coastal neighbors, is characterized by a subsistence lifestyle. In March the village is also characterized by huge, hardened snowdrifts, some of them dozens of feet long and higher than your head, that have built up during the long winter.

Two of the Iditarod's most memorable and inspirational episodes

Jerry Austin gives his dogs a whitefish snack during an unusually calm day along the coast in 1987. The team has just come through the Blueberry Hills (in the background) between Unalakleet and Shaktoolik.

began in Shaktoolik. The first was in 1982, when a raging blizzard forced a temporary halt to the race. More than a dozen mushers congregated in Shaktoolik rather than travel through the storm to Koyuk, 58 trail miles north. To reach the next checkpoint, teams would have to cross ice-covered Norton Bay, which offers no protection from the wind. The bay is also a notoriously difficult place to follow the trail; markings are often moved by shifting ice or knocked down by gale-force blasts and buried by snow.

One musher refused to play it safe. Herbie Nayokpuk, a noted ivory carver and musher from the Eskimo village of Shishmaref, had been a perennial contender since the early 1970s but never won the championship. Sensing that the halt in the race might be his chance for victory, he left the warmth and safety of Shaktoolik and drove his dogs into the storm. "It was good weather for me," he later explained. "I've gone out in worse weather than that. I would have made it easy if I'd just gone out two hours earlier."

The "Shishmaref Cannonball" (a name he earned for his shot-out-of-a-cannon mushing style) departed at noon and made good progress for about five hours. But after he had traveled 22 miles, the winds increased to 60 miles per hour and the visibility became so poor that neither he nor the dogs could follow the trail. Deciding it would be foolish to continue on, he stopped the team and climbed into his sleeping bag, which he put inside the sled bag. Sleep, however, was impossible: "The sled was real small and I had to kind of sit. I was real wet. I was just shivering in there."

Three snowmobilers from Koyuk went looking for Nayokpuk and

found him at 1:00 A.M. They waited for daybreak to move. But in the morning, the storm was so fierce that the group chose to retreat to Shaktoolik, rather than face into the gale. Even traveling with the wind they had great difficulty following the trail; at one point the men searched more than an hour for markers. After finally reaching the checkpoint, Nayokpuk all but admitted defeat. "I really ruined my dogs when I couldn't find the trail," he lamented. "I think they're bummed out." As Nayokpuk feared, the unsuccessful run took a heavy toll. When the storm finally let up, his team no longer had the stamina or enthusiasm to keep up with the leaders. Swenson ended up winning the race; the Cannonball placed twelfth.

Three years later, another musher took a chance similar to Nayokpuk's. But this time the gamble worked. And it led to the "Legend of Libby." As Dean Osmar had done the previous year, Libby Riddles entered

John Cooper crosses Norton Bay, between Shaktoolik and Koyuk, during the 1985 Iditarod. The trail is marked by small spruce trees; villagers chop holes in the ice and insert the spruce, which then freeze in place.

Sled dogs curl up in 30-mile-per-hour winds at the Safety checkpoint. Naturally equipped to sleep in such harsh weather, they curl up, with their tails across their faces, and become buried by snow, which adds another layer of insulation to their fur coats.

Unalakleet to Nome

Libby Riddles smiles at the beginning of the 1989 Iditarod. Four years earlier, Libby became the first woman to win the race after crossing Norton Bay in the midst of a severe blizzard.

the 1985 Iditarod as a dark horse. A 28-year-old resident of Teller, a small coastal town about 70 miles north of Nome, Riddles had placed eighteenth and twentieth in her two previous Iditarod appearances. Outside racing circles, she was a virtual unknown. Even within the mushing community, she was clearly overshadowed by Susan Butcher, the most prominent female in Iditarod history.

Riddles had more than her share of problems early in the race. First the brake on her sled busted, then her team got away. Fortunately, neither incident proved disastrous. A replacement brake was quickly found, and Riddles caught her runaway dogs before any was injured, thanks to the assistance of two competitors, Chuck Schaeffer and Terry Adkins.

Then, just when things were starting to look up, several dogs became infected with viral diarrhea. "It's disgusting when they get sick," she later commented. "They're not eating and not able to work. You have to give

Iditarod: The Great Race to Nome

them long periods of rest." Luckily for Riddles, the team got lengthy, unplanned rest breaks when race officials ordered the freezes at both Rainy Pass and McGrath. "That really worked out well for me," she admitted. "The dogs recovered nicely." (Butcher wasn't nearly so lucky; this was the year a moose attack forced her from the race.)

Despite her early woes, Riddles gradually worked her way to the front of the pack and was in excellent position as the race hit the coast. She reached Unalakleet in second place, two hours behind Lavon Barve of Wasilla, and was the first musher to leave the checkpoint.

Riddles drove into Shaktoolik at 2:17 in the afternoon, in the middle of a severe storm. Despite winds that gusted to more than 40 miles per hour and near whiteout conditions, Riddles at least had the option of heading across Norton Bay in daylight. Her rivals wouldn't arrive until evening. And none would choose to challenge the storm in darkness.

Even with daylight to help her find the trail, Riddles had second thoughts. She called up then–kennel partner Joe Garnie, who'd finished third in the 1984 race, and asked for advice. Garnie said "Go." So did two other people whose opinions she respected. So Riddles pointed her team north and headed into the storm. Gusting winds now blowing up to 60 miles per hour created a ground blizzard as she left Shaktoolik. But conditions soon got even worse. Whiteout conditions made it nearly impossible to follow the trail, and wind-chill temperatures dropped to minus 50 degrees and below.

"As soon as we left town, it went from being a race to a survival test," Riddles later said. "But I'd already made up my mind that if I couldn't get across, I'd camp. There's nothing more depressing than backtracking. You lose all those miles you've gained. And the next time you leave a checkpoint, the dogs are real reluctant to go. They remember the negative experience." For two and a half hours, Riddles drove her team ahead, plowing through blinding snow. Stakes marking the trail were the dogs' only guide. Finally, with darkness setting in, Riddles made camp to keep from getting lost. It was impossible to determine the team's location. Only one thing was certain: there was no place to take shelter.

For the dogs, this presented no real problem. They curled up, their tails across their faces, and were quickly buried by snow, which added further insulation to their fur coats. But for Riddles, the hardest and most frightening part of her 24-hour crossing was about to begin. She had to change out of her wet outer clothing before climbing inside the sleeping bag. "It was a real effort. I had to take off my fur parka and almost got frostbit hands doing that. Then I realized I had to take off my snowpants too. So I had to

Libby Riddles, with her winning lead dogs Axle and Dugan, holds roses and a bottle of champagne after reaching Nome in first place in 1985.

go through the whole process again. Finally I got into my sleeping bag. I knew that as long as I had warm, dry clothing, I'd be OK."

Still, there was fear. Riddles was scared of frostbite, scared of hypothermia, scared of freezing to death. "You'd have to be stupid if you weren't scared in those conditions," she said. "It was probably the most dangerous position I've ever been in. But fear helps keep things in proper perspective. And I just kept telling myself, if you win the race it's worth it."

Riddles bundled herself as well as possible. She pulled over the fur-lined parka hood, and when her neckwarmer froze, she used dog booties as face warmers. She stayed in her sleeping bag for 10 hours or more, until there was enough daylight to travel. After a breakfast of seal oil and Norwegian chocolate, she resumed the trek.

From the camping spot, it was another 45 to 50 miles to Koyuk. Riddles stopped the team occasionally, to get her bearings. Finally, just as darkness was again approaching, she spotted the village. After being mobbed by its residents, she officially checked in at 5:13 P.M., nearly a full day after leaving Shaktoolik. Libby's gamble had worked. Now only 171 miles from Nome, her nearest competitors were more than six hours behind.

Through her gamble and ensuing victory, Libby Riddles became the star of the Iditarod show, Alaska's "first lady of mushing." In a matter of days, she'd gone from unknown to nationally known. Along the way, she blazed new trails for the Iditarod's publicity-hungry organizers while earning accolades and honors no male musher had ever before received.

After crossing Norton Bay, the race route bends to the west while following the Seward Peninsula's southern coastline. Beyond Koyuk, mushers travel through three more tiny Eskimo settlements: Elim (population about 220), Golovin (120), and White Mountain (150). Although their sojourns in the first two communities are usually short ones, mushers are required to take a six-hour layover at White Mountain. This mandatory stop (expanded from four to six hours in 1989) ensures that the dogs will get at least one extended rest over the final miles.

From White Mountain, only one checkpoint—Safety, which is 22 miles from race's end—and 77 miles separate Iditarod teams from Nome. Several heart-pounding sprints to the finish have been staged over this final stretch of trail. From 1973 to 1991, the Iditarod champion and runners-up were separated by less than an hour on seven occasions. Three times the winning edge was less than five minutes. And in one remarkable race, a single tick of the clock separated first place from second.

One of the most memorable duels of the past decade took place in

1986, when Susan Butcher of Eureka and Joe Garnie of Teller raced neck-and-neck down the homestretch in a battle of sentimental favorites. Both, in their own ways, were underdogs. Much of Alaska was rooting for Butcher. Though she'd placed second in several previous sled dog races, including two runner-up finishes in the Iditarod, Susan had never taken top honors in a major event.

Garnie, meanwhile, was trying to duplicate the feat of then-partner Libby Riddles, who one year earlier had raced into Iditarod lore with her fairytale victory. If he won, the Riddles-Garnie kennel would be the first to capture back-to-back Iditarods since Swenson in 1981–82. Even more impressive, he would symbolize the hopes and dreams of all small-kennel owners, by upsetting a musher who'd devoted her life to dog racing and turned it into a major, year-round business.

Then the mayor of Teller, Garnie was especially popular in Northwest Alaska. Like Riddles, he was a resident of the region. He was also an

Tim Osmar mushes his team past one of the few trees growing along the Bering Sea coast during the 1987 Iditarod. Two different types of trail markers are visible: a driftwood tripod and red flagging.

Dewey Halverson's team travels on the ice of Norton Sound after leaving Elim in 1983. The spruce tree on his left is a trail marker.

Eskimo and thus could become the first Native winner since Jerry Riley a decade earlier.

Finally, there was the matter of Garnie's persistence. He'd put himself in a position to win despite some bad luck earlier in the race. Twice his team had gotten off the Iditarod Trail. He'd lost a few hours the first night of the race, then made a wrong turn between McGrath and Takotna, a mistake that cost him the lead as well as another four hours of time. He'd also busted a couple of sleds. "It's to the point where I'm beyond shock when something like this happens," he said. Fortunately, in both instances, Garnie was able to borrow another sled and stay in the chase.

From Unalakleet to Safety, no more than a few minutes separated Butcher and Garnie as they arrived and departed checkpoints. Almost always within sight, they closely watched each other's teams, trying to gauge their relative strengths. After reaching White Mountain only four minutes apart, both mushers gave Butcher the edge. "I don't know about speed. I think my team can keep up with anybody's. But as far as being tired, there's no question Susan's has had more rest," Garnie said.

After resting at White Mountain, the teams pushed on to Safety, where Butcher owned a nine-minute lead. But as both mushers had anticipated, Garnie's come-from-way-behind push had forced his team to use up its reserves. Over the final 22 miles, Butcher pulled away to win the 1986 Iditarod by more than 55 minutes. "It's a relief to win and get it over with," she admitted. "Now I don't have to worry about it anymore."

Though Butcher has been involved in several coastal sprints since the early 1980s, neither she nor any other Iditarod musher comes close to matching Swenson's record for dramatic finishes. All of his wins have been close ones. Four of his five victories have been by less than an hour, and twice he's won by less than five minutes: in 1977, he beat Jerry Riley by four minutes, 52 seconds; in '82, he edged Butcher by 3:43. Only once has Swenson lost a close decision. Ironically, it was the most dramatic and controversial finish in Iditarod history. After more than 14 days of howling winds, ground blizzards, numbing cold, and sleep deprivation, Wasilla musher Dick Mackey beat Swenson by one second.

Mackey entered the 1978 Iditarod with impressive credentials. One of only two men (Ken Chase of Anvik was the other) to finish each of the first five races to Nome, he'd been a perennial top 10 finisher, but had never been number one. Swenson had run only two previous Iditarods, but already wore the title of champion, following his 1977 victory.

Mackey figured that Swenson was again the musher to beat in 1978, so his strategy was simple: stay close to Rick. Throughout the Interior and along the Bering Sea coast, he did just that. Pushing hard to remain with Swenson, Mackey slept little, maybe 10 hours over the final week of racing. But his strategy worked. At Safety, 22 miles from Nome, Mackey shared the lead with Swenson. It was, as he'd hoped, a two-team race.

In Nome, people began talking of a dead heat, a photo finish, as updates periodically filtered in. With nine miles to go, Mackey held a two-mile lead. It seemed he was pulling away. But with four miles remaining, Swenson had regained the lead, though only by the length of his team.

Above: *Joe Garnie reaches the finish line in Nome just ahead of Libby Riddles in 1989. The former partners finished just one minute and 12 seconds apart.*
Below: *Dog teams arrive at White Mountain, where mushers are required to take a six-hour layover before completing the final 77 miles to Nome.*

Above: *The crowd lining
Nome's Front Street cheers on
an Iditarod finisher.*
Below: *Runner-up Martin
Buser gives his dogs a much
deserved thank-you at the end
of the 1991 race.*
Opposite: *Rick Swenson poses
with lead dog Goose shortly
after winning a record fifth
Iditarod crown in 1991.*

As the town's siren blared, signaling the teams' arrival, spectators crowded the fences that line Nome's 50-yard-long finishing chute. Through the dawn light, Swenson and Mackey pushed their dogs up Front Street toward the burled spruce arch that marks the Iditarod's end. According to a newspaper account:

All eyes stared down the street, as the distant figures focused.

"They're dead even," someone shouted as the mushers stormed the chute.

Mackey's whip cracked. Swenson bore down.

Roars went up and people screamed the teams to the line. It was over. But few knew who had won.

Swenson's sled was over the line, resting a few feet in front of Mackey's, with six dogs in harness. But Mackey's team of eight was stretched further forward. Mackey fell from his sled, collapsing on the ground. His wife flew to his side.

The mushers disappeared under the deluge of press, race officials, and family. Voices croaked. Confusion reigned.

"It's the first dog across the line that determines the winner," race marshal Myron Gavin said. "The winner is Dick Mackey."

The crowd's roar hit a crescendo. Icicles frozen into his mustache, his eyes glazed and glassy, his mind rummy from no sleep, Mackey understood. He had won the 1978 Iditarod Trail Sled Dog Race, riding in at 6:52 A.M. on a sparkling, crystal-blue morning. . . .

"It's about time," the 45-year-old musher said. "It's been a dream of mine for six years now."

Thinking that he had earned the victory, Swenson waved to the crowd after crossing the finish line. When notified of the race marshal's decision, he handled what had become an upsetting loss in style. According to a second newspaper report, "Swenson didn't rant and rave. He didn't complain. 'If you made a decision, stick by it,' he told the race marshal. Swenson kept a smile on his sunburned face and his thoughts to himself."

Though the winners draw the biggest crowds and earn the most attention, all mushers—and dogs—who reach Nome are treated as champions. Their arrival signaled by the town's siren, even the back-of-the-packers receive an official welcome, and they're greeted by a faithful core of friends and fans who offer applause and congratulations. All finishers are honored at post-race banquets and awarded brass belt buckles and special patches that reflect their personal victories.

Iditarod: The Great Race to Nome

Unalakleet to Nome

FOR EVERY BUTCHER and Swenson and Riddles, there are a dozen mushers who enter the Iditarod simply to find adventure and test their limits. That search is ultimately what accounts for the Iditarod's great popularity. Perhaps one of the Iditarod's greatest achievements is the manner in which it has rekindled an interest in mushing throughout Alaska, while helping to unify the state. But for all of us, the race celebrates the adventurous spirit associated with America's Last Frontier. The past and the present are annually reunited along the Iditarod Trail.

As Joe Redington, Sr., explained back in the late 1970s: "I would like to say something on what makes you run the Iditarod. I think it's a certain type of person that wants to explore. . . . My dad, when he was 14 years old, rode a horse into the Oklahoma Territory, looking for something. I don't know what. But you're looking for something different, and the Iditarod is the last place you can prove to yourself that you've got something your forefathers had."

Notes

The majority of material in the text, especially quoted material from Iditarod participants, has been gathered by the author over a period of years as a reporter with *The Anchorage Times* or taken from newspaper accounts of the Iditarod. Other important sources for the three first sections of the book are described below.

The Gold Rush Era

The Bureau of Land Management carried out an *Iditarod Trail Oral History Project* in 1980–81. Taped interviews were conducted with old-timers who lived along the trail, mushers who ran in the 1925 diphtheria run, and other persons closely connected with the trail at various times. The tapes are available at many Alaska libraries. Some information given in the first section of the book, such as Pete Curran, Bill McCarty, and Edgar Kalland's remarks, is taken from the BLM tapes.

The All-Alaska Sweepstakes

The main source for Scotty Allan's story was Shannon Garst's *Scotty Allan, King of the Dog Team Drivers* (1946). Other information on issues such as treatment of dogs can be found in Esther Birdsall Darling's 1916 booklet, *The Great Dog Races of Nome*.

The Race for Life

The primary source of information for the 1925 Serum Run was Kenneth Ungermann's 1963 *The Race to Nome*. The relay sequence list and related text discussion are slightly different from that given in Ungermann's book and are based on more recent information provided by Edgar Kalland in a 1980 interview, conducted as part of the BLM's *Iditarod Trail Oral History Project*.

Overleaf: *Tim Osmar's team is silhouetted against the setting sun while mushing toward the village of Unalakleet.*
Opposite: *Peter Thomann struggles to keep his sled upright as his team winds down ice-covered Dalzell Creek during the 1987 race. The icy trail makes it difficult for mushers to control their teams.*

Iditarod: The Great Race to Nome

Guy Blankenship mushes down the wind-scoured South Fork of the Kuskokwim River shortly after leaving the Rohn checkpoint during the 1986 race.

Iditarod Champions 1973 to 1991

YEAR	MUSHER/HOMETOWN	WINNING TIME (days/hr/min/sec)
1973	Dick Wilmarth, Red Devil	20:00:49:41
1974	Carl Huntington, Galena	20:15:02:07
1975	Emmitt Peters, Ruby	14:14:43:45
1976	Gerald Riley, Nenana	18:22:58:17
1977	Rick Swenson, Eureka	16:16:27:13
1978	Dick Mackey, Wasilla	14:18:52:24
1979	Rick Swenson, Eureka	15:10:37:47
1980	Joe May, Trapper Creek	14:07:11:51
1981	Rick Swenson, Eureka	12:08:45:02
1982	Rick Swenson, Eureka	16:04:40:10
1983	Rick Mackey, Wasilla	12:14:10:14
1984	Dean Osmar, Clam Gulch	12:15:07:33
1985	Libby Riddles, Teller	18:00:20:17
1986	Susan Butcher, Eureka	11:15:06:00
1987	Susan Butcher, Eureka	11:02:05:13
1988	Susan Butcher, Eureka	11:11:41:40
1989	Joe Runyan, Nenana	11:05:24:34
1990	Susan Butcher, Eureka	11:01:53:23
1991	Rick Swenson, Two Rivers	12:16:34:39

PLACE	1973	1991
1	$12,000	$50,000
2	8,000	39,500
3	6,000	32,000
4	4,000	24,500
5	3,000	19,000
6	2,500	15,000
7	2,000	14,000
8	1,800	13,000
9	1,600	12,000
10	1,400	11,000
11	1,000	9,500
12	950	9,000
13	900	8,500
14	850	8,000
15	800	7,500
16	750	6,500
17	700	6,000
18	650	5,500
19	600	5,000
20	500	4,500
Total Purse $50,000		**$300,000**

**Iditarod Purses
1973 and 1991**

Note: In 1991, each musher finishing below twentieth place received $1,000.

Iditarod: The Great Race to Nome

141

Bibliography

Anchorage Daily News and *The Anchorage Times,* miscellaneous staff and Associated Press reports from 1973 through 1991.

Bureau of Land Management. *Iditarod Trail Oral History Project* (tapes). Anchorage: U.S. Department of the Interior, 1980-81.

Bureau of Land Management. *The Iditarod National Historic Trail, Seward to Nome Route, A Comprehensive Management Plan.* Anchorage: U.S. Department of the Interior, 1986.

Cadwallader, Charles Lee. *Reminiscences of the Iditarod Trail.* n.p., n.d.

Cellura, Dominique. *Travelers of the Cold: Sled Dogs of the Far North.* Bothell, Washington: Alaska Northwest Books™, 1990.

Coppinger, Lorna. *The World of Sled Dogs, From Siberia to Sport Racing.* New York: Howell Book House, 1982.

Darling, Esther Birdsall. *Baldy of Nome.* Philadelphia: Penn Publishing Co., 1916.

———. *The Great Dog Races of Nome, Official Souvenir History* (1916). Knik: Iditarod Trail Committee, 1969.

Dogs of the North. Anchorage: Alaska Geographic Society, 1987.

Garst, Shannon. *Scotty Allan, King of the Dog Team Drivers.* New York: Julian Messner, 1946.

Hart, Betsy. *The History of Ruby, Alaska, "The Gem of the Yukon."* Anchorage: National Bilingual Center, no date.

Iditarod Press Packet. Wasilla: Iditarod Trail Committee, 1989 and 1990.

Jones, Tim. *The Last Great Race.* Seattle: Madrona Publishers, 1982.

Nielsen, Nicki J. *The Iditarod: Women on the Trail.* Anchorage: Wolfdog Publications, 1986.

Page, Dorothy. *Iditarod Trail Annual, Anchorage to Nome Race,* 1974 to 1986 editions.

Richer, Elizabeth M. *Seppala: Alaska Dog Driver.* Boston: Little, Brown & Co., 1930.

Riddles, Libby, and Tim Jones. *The Race Across Alaska.* Harrisburg, Penn.: Stackpole Books, 1988.

Stuck, Hudson. *Ten Thousand Miles with a Dog Sled* (1914). Lincoln, Nebraska: University of Nebraska Press, 1988.

Thompson, Raymond. *Seppala's Saga of the Sled Dog.* Lynnwood, Wash., n.d.

Ungermann, Kenneth A. *The Race to Nome.* New York: Harper & Row, 1963.

Vaudrin, Bill. *Racing Alaskan Sled Dogs.* Anchorage: Alaska Northwest Publishing Co., 1976,

Wendt, Ron. *Alaska Dog Mushing Guide.* Anchorage: Alaska/Yukon Publications, 1987.

Wickersham, The Honorable James. *Old Yukon Tales, Trails and Trials.* Washington D.C.: Washington Law Book Co., 1938.